Stoicism: A Very Short Introduction

VERY SHORT INTRODUCTIONS are for anyone wanting a stimulating and accessible way into a new subject. They are written by experts, and have been translated into more than 45 different languages.

The series began in 1995, and now covers a wide variety of topics in every discipline. The VSI library currently contains over 550 volumes—a Very Short Introduction to everything from Psychology and Philosophy of Science to American History and Relativity—and continues to grow in every subject area.

Very Short Introductions available now:

Available soon:

For more information visit our website

www.oup.com/vsi/

Brad Inwood

STOICISM

A Very Short Introduction

OXFORD
UNIVERSITY PRESS

OXFORD

UNIVERSITY PRESS

Great Clarendon Street, Oxford, OX2 6DP,
United Kingdom

Oxford University Press is a department of the University of Oxford.
It furthers the University's objective of excellence in research, scholarship,
and education by publishing worldwide. Oxford is a registered trade mark of
Oxford University Press in the UK and in certain other countries

© Brad Inwood 2018

The moral rights of the author have been asserted

First edition published in 2018

Published in the United States of America by Oxford University Press
198 Madison Avenue, New York, NY 10016, United States of America

British Library Cataloguing in Publication Data
Data available

Library of Congress Control Number: 2018934170

ISBN 978-0-19-878666-5

Printed and bound by
CPI Group (UK) Ltd, Croydon, CR0 4YY

Contents

Acknowledgements

I've been reading, talking, and writing about Stoicism for a long time, and so I have accumulated more debts than I could begin to count, debts owed to teachers, colleagues, students, friends, and family members. For this project, I owe special thanks to three friends who read and advised me on an earlier version of the book: Ryan Balot and John Magee in Toronto, and Raphael Woolf in London. Their insights helped me to improve the book in many ways and for that, as well as for precious intellectual comradeship, I thank them all warmly. I am also grateful to the editors at OUP and their anonymous reader for helping to keep the project on track. My deepest gratitude, though, is to my wife, Niko Scharer, *sine qua non*.

List of illustrations

Chapter 1
Ancient Stoicism and modern life

> Before you get going in the morning say to yourself, 'Today I'll meet people who are meddlers, ingrates, bullies, cheaters, envious and antisocial people. All of this happens because they don't know the difference between what's good and what's bad.'
>
> (Marcus Aurelius, *To Himself* 2.1)

What a way to start the day! And yet it's probably true for many of us, most days. Unless you live a charmed life, you are likely to come up against a certain amount of distressing unpleasantness, much of it coming from your fellow human beings. Marcus Aurelius, emperor of Rome, faced this dismal fact head on; the quotation above is the first bit of advice he gave himself in his philosophical diary. It's not exactly what most of us would describe as uplifting. To be fair, Marcus often had very bad days—his life was littered with war, plague, betrayal, and hard times—and an emperor is the man that everyone wants something from. So it wouldn't be surprising if he reacted like Marvin, the paranoid android in *The Hitchhiker's Guide to the Galaxy*: 'It's the people you meet in this job that really get you down.'

Marvin reacted with persistently low spirits, but Marcus did not. One major reason for this difference—aside from the fact that Marvin was a fictional robot and Marcus was a real human being—is that Marcus Aurelius, emperor of Rome from 161 to 180 CE and arguably the most powerful man alive at the time, was also a Stoic. And Stoicism, as is well-known, prepares its adherents for the tough times, gives them perspective, puts things in context. If life hands out lemons, the Stoic will certainly *try* making lemonade, but if that doesn't work she'll at least know why and be able to manage nicely. Her philosophy prepares her for whatever the world sends her way; she will be well-practised in the art of managing life, using her intelligence and training to embrace it, whether it's going well or badly. Her philosophy will be a genuine guide for life.

The academic honour society ΦΒΚ (Phi Beta Kappa) takes its name from this conception; the Greek letters stand for *philosophia biou kubernētēs* 'philosophy is the steersman of life', and there could hardly be a better summary of what Stoicism stands for in the eyes of most people today. In the western tradition the idea of philosophy as a way of life, or at least the principal guide for life, is far older than ΦΒΚ (founded 1776) itself. It began with Greek philosophy, certainly no later than Socrates and quite possibly as early as Pythagoras, and has persisted in one form or another ever since. In the ancient world of the Greeks and Romans the thought had its fullest and clearest development in Stoicism. Even today the idea that philosophy can be the guide to a good life maintains a very strong connection to this ancient school of thought, though of course in a modern guise. A recent volume of posts from the blog *Stoicism Today* (volume 2, 2016, edited by Patrick Ussher with Tom McConnell) contains articles with titles such as:

- 'Stoicism and the Environment'
- 'How Does the Stoic Tweet?'
- '"Barbarians at the Gates": Stoic Responses to the Refugee Crisis'
- 'How to Become Virtuous—Lessons from Compassion Focussed Therapy (CFT)'
- 'The Internet and the Dinner Party: Cultivating Stoic Calm in the Online World'

And that is just scratching the surface of what Stoicism is thought to offer by way of guidance for life in the 21st century. Some relatively recent books underline the point: Elen Buzaré's *Stoic Spiritual Exercises* (explicitly building on the work of Pierre Hadot) and Donald Robertson's *Stoicism and the Art of Happiness* (the author is a psychotherapist specializing in cognitive-behavioural therapy and has published an essay in *Stoicism Today*: 'Providence or Atoms? Atoms! A Defence of Being a Modern Stoic Atheist'). Add to that *The Daily Stoic* website and the book of the same title by Ryan Holiday and Stephen Hanselman offering sage advice for every day of the year and it seems that Stoicism is all around us.

The 20th-century French philosopher and scholar, Pierre Hadot, believed that philosophy as we have inherited it from the ancient world is still a viable, indeed indispensable, way of life. Though he argued (controversially and from a broadly existentialist perspective) that virtually all the ancient Greek schools treated philosophy as a way of life in roughly the same sense, Hadot made Stoicism the foundation of his argument and treated Marcus Aurelius as the best exemplification of this aspect of the school, followed closely by the former Greek slave, Epictetus, who had been a major philosophical inspiration for Marcus. (In a very different intellectual tradition, John Cooper makes a broadly similar case in his 2012 book *The Pursuits of Wisdom*.) Marcus and Epictetus, Roman and Greek, emperor and slave: what better symbolism could there be for the universal appeal of philosophy as a guide to life, and in fact to the best way of life? (See Box 1.)

As popular as Marcus has been in recent centuries, the career of Epictetus as an icon of this way of looking at philosophy began even earlier. His 'Discourses', written up and published by one of his students, inspired popular philosophical lecturers for a century after his death. This was probably what led to Marcus' discovery of them. In book one of his diary (an introduction that summarizes with gratitude what he learned from the many influences in his

Box 1 Epitectus and Marcus Aurelius

Epictetus was born in Hierapolis in Phrygia (Asia Minor) around 50 CE and sent to Rome as a slave while still young. His master was a Greek freedman, Epaphroditus, who served at Nero's court. Epictetus studied philosophy with Musonius Rufus, was eventually freed, and then was expelled from Rome by Domitian along with other teachers of philosophy. He set up a school in Nicopolis, in north-western Greece, where he taught until his death early in the 2nd century CE. He lectured on technical topics in Stoicism, but also delivered more accessible public lectures which form the basis of the *Discourses* reported by his student Arrian.

Marcus Aurelius was born to a politically important aristocratic family in 121 CE and had an exceptional education in rhetoric, philosophy, and politics. Preferring the philosophical life, he was nevertheless adopted as successor to the emperor Antoninus Pius. After a long apprenticeship in power, he became emperor in 161 CE and governed well under difficult circumstances until his death (while on military campaign) in 180 CE. He established philosophical schools in Athens during his reign. His philosophical diary, *To Himself* (more commonly known as the *Meditations*), wasn't published in his lifetime and became influential when it was 'rediscovered' in the 10th century CE.

life), Marcus says that he was introduced to Epictetus' thought by his friend and mentor Quintus Junius Rusticus (*To Himself* 1.7). An eminent Platonist of late antiquity, Simplicius, thought that the compact *Handbook* of extracts from Epictetus was important enough for a massive commentary. Medieval Christians adapted his work to their own confessional aims and then the Renaissance virtually exploded with translations and adaptations. In the 20th century, his work inspired novelist Tom Wolfe (*A Man in Full*, published in 1998) and the American fighter pilot James

Stockdale to reflect on the practical value of Stoicism as a guide for life in the modern world (in an essay in *The Atlantic* in 1978). Various kinds of psychotherapy lay claim to an affinity with Epictetus' brand of philosophy, from the logotherapy of Viktor Frankl to Albert Ellis's rational emotive therapy.

Let's turn back to Marcus for a moment to get a sense of the kind of thinking he recommends. Recall that the reason he suggests for all that annoying anti-social behaviour from people is that they don't know the difference between what's good and what's bad. He continues:

> But I have seen that the nature of the good is the honourable and the nature of the bad is the shameful, and that the nature of the wrongdoer himself is akin to me. He doesn't share the same blood or seed, but he does share in reason and a portion of the divine. Having seen that, I cannot be harmed by any of those people. For no one can enmesh me in what is shameful. And I cannot get angry at my kinsman nor can I be hostile to him. For we are born for cooperation, like hands, like feet, like eyelids and the rows of upper and lower teeth. So acting against one another is contrary to nature. And annoyance and rejection amount to acting against one another.

Evidently Marcus thinks that we can cope best with the challenges presented by antisocial bullies, for example, if we keep some basic facts in mind.

First, their problem is that they don't know right from wrong. If they did, they would surely act better. As Socrates said, no one does wrong willingly, and presumably the thing to do is to *teach* such people rather than to get angry or vengeful. Socrates acted on his own advice: at his trial (*Apology* 26a) he suggested that his prosecutor should be teaching him what is right rather than prosecuting him for his alleged mistakes, but the jury was not convinced.

Second, Marcus himself *does* understand what is good and bad. What I have here translated as 'honourable' is the Greek word (yes, the Roman emperor wrote his notebook in Greek) *kalon*, often rendered as 'fine' or 'beautiful' or 'noble'. Its opposite is the 'shameful' (*aischron*), something ugly, either physically or morally, and Marcus' point is that nothing anyone else does can subject us to that. This too is a Socratic idea, and for over 500 years philosophers had been relying on Socrates' arguments to reach this conclusion. Marcus thinks that just knowing what is genuinely good and bad will give him the perspective he needs to tolerate his fellow human beings.

The third reflection is that they are indeed *fellow* human beings, kinsmen, in fact; not literally family members (as those who share blood and genetic material would be), but part of a family defined by a shared possession of rationality, which is a kind of divine gift. These oafs I meet may be objectionable, but they are family. Why should that matter? Marcus finally invokes a key fact about human nature: we are built for cooperation within the family of rational beings. As our left and right hands are made to work together, as our upper and lower molars are designed for a shared purpose, so each of us has a nature that is built for working together with our relations in the family of reason. If our hands don't cooperate they are frustrating their natural purpose; so too for upper and lower teeth. And, if the analogy holds, we would be just as much out of harmony with our own nature if we acted against family members. So if Marcus gets annoyed at or turns his back on those sycophantic wheedlers and bullies he will be frustrating something in his own rational nature.

This is the sort of thinking that Pierre Hadot called a 'spiritual exercise', borrowing the term from a later and overtly religious tradition; he invokes Ignatius Loyola explicitly in *Philosophy as a Way of Life* (pp. 82, 126) and also compares ancient philosophical practice to certain monastic exercises. This kind of thinking certainly admits of being treated that way. One could imagine Marcus rising for his philosophical devotions and reciting:

1. Today I'll meet with annoying fools.
2. But they don't know what they're doing, and I do.
3. They are my kinsmen in reason.
4. Kinsmen in reason are built to work together.
5. So it's in my nature to work with them rather than dismiss them angrily.

This would no doubt brace him for the inevitable, and make the frustrations of dealing with greedy and envious courtiers easier to bear. Alternatively, one could imagine him skipping the morning recitation routine but always having this line of thought ready to deploy at a moment's notice, as soon as some importunate thug appears. This is advice that another Stoic involved in political life gives; Nero's adviser, Seneca, credits a contemporary Cynic philosopher with making the point (*On Benefits* 7.1.3–7.2.1). At any rate, if Marcus makes enough of a habit of this and similar reflections, he'll develop a way of being in the world that protects him from negative emotions. There you have it, Stoicism at work. For another such exercise, take a look at the end of the first chapter of Epictetus' *Handbook*.

> Examine each impression and test it by the standards that you possess: first and foremost ask whether it deals with things in our power or with those that aren't; and if it deals with things not in our power keep ready to hand the thought, 'it is nothing to me'.

In the 20th century, the heroic American fighter pilot, James Stockdale, was shot down over North Vietnam and imprisoned under brutal conditions for the duration of the war. He writes about applying what he remembered of Epictetus' *Handbook* from his studies at Stanford University (he considers it a 'book of military ethics') to the situation he found himself in when he 'left the land of technology' and 'entered the world of Epictetus'.

Stockdale never mentions daily recitations or his 'exercises', but he claims to have survived psychologically only because he remembered key lessons from the book.

> In Palo Alto, I had read this book, not with contentment, but with annoyance. Statement after statement: 'Men are disturbed not by things, but by the view that they take of them.' 'Do not be concerned with things which are beyond your power.' 'Demand not that events should happen as you wish, but wish them to happen as they do happen and you will go on well.' This is stoicism. It's not the last word, but it's a viewpoint that comes in handy in many circumstances, and it surely did for me. Particularly this line: 'Lameness is an impediment to the body but not to the will.' That was significant for me because I wasn't able to stand up and support myself on my badly broken leg for the first couple of years I was in solitary confinement.

Stockdale is referring to the fact that Epictetus himself was lame in one leg, allegedly because of mistreatment by his master. When faced with the temptation to collaborate with his captors in return for better treatment, Stockdale recalled:

> The old stoic had said, 'If I can get the things I need with the preservation of my honor and fidelity and self-respect, show me the way and I will get them. But, if you require me to lose my own proper good, that you may gain what is no good, consider how unreasonable and foolish you are.' To love our fellow prisoners was within our power. To betray, to propagandize, to disillusion conscientious and patriotic shipmates and destroy their morale so that they in turn would be destroyed was to lose one's proper good.

Stockdale the fighter pilot saw himself as a man of war. 'I'm a fighter pilot. I'm a technical man. I'm a test pilot. I know how to get people to do technical work. I play golf; I drink martinis. I know how to get ahead in my profession.' A man could hardly be more different from the French intellectual, Pierre Hadot, a

8

former priest and existentialist teaching at the Collège de France in the circle of Michel Foucault. Stockdale doesn't think of his Stoicism as a set of spiritual exercises. He writes bluntly of remembering what he read in a book assigned to him in college and finding it useful in the field. He was grateful for being pushed to read it and grateful for the resources he could find in what he remembered, thoughts and attitudes that enabled him to maintain his sanity and integrity under years of torture and isolation. No spiritual mantras here, but a frank assessment of what works psychologically.

Epictetus, the Greek slave and professional teacher, and Marcus, the Roman emperor and military commander, were as different from each other as were Hadot and Stockdale. It is a curious accident perhaps that the French intellectual focused most intently on the Roman general, while the American fighter pilot drew on the words of the lowly Greek philosopher. The breadth of Stoicism's appeal could hardly be more clearly illustrated. But there is something very important that Hadot and Stockdale have in common. Both apply Stoicism as they understand it to life; it is a matter of having recourse to set lessons to help manage life, rather than an open-ended enquiry into the way the world works. Hadot is at times quite frank about his belief that the underlying theories don't matter to philosophy as a way of life, claiming that the spiritual exercises come first and the doctrines are worked up later to support them (*Philosophy as a Way of Life*, p. 282). Stockdale doesn't even mention underlying doctrines in physics, logic, and ethics—he wouldn't have found any in the *Handbook* and it served his purpose well just as he remembered it.

This view of Stoicism as a practical psychological aid is probably the commonest current approach to the school in our own society. But there is another conception of Stoicism that we should also consider, one that puts more emphasis on its historical origins and on the underlying theoretical work that led to the development of Stoic philosophy in the ancient world and provided *reasons* for adopting their views rather than those of other therapeutic philosophies. There is a striking gap between the current understanding of Stoicism as a therapeutic psychological endeavour, or at least a practical philosophical strategy, and what you would meet if you plunged into contemporary academic writing about the ancient school. Modern research on the school focuses on its history, especially its early history (both Epictetus and Marcus wrote in the final phase of the school's long development; Marcus, almost 500 years after its foundation), its interaction and debates with other philosophical schools, and the detailed reconstruction of its doctrines and philosophical methods. It's not exactly a surprise that professional academic writing on a topic should be different from work that is designed to be more widely accessible, but in the case of Stoicism the gap is quite a bit wider than one would normally expect.

One of the reasons for this gap is suggested by the word 'reconstruction' that I just used. To get a sense of what is at stake here we need to begin with some historical details and hard facts about our knowledge of some ancient philosophical movements. First the time line. As Figure 1 summarizes, the Stoic school had a long history, from its foundation at some point very late in the 4th century BCE (perhaps between 310 and 300; no exact record survives) until the early years of the 3rd century CE (perhaps around 220 CE). But the first complete work of Stoic philosophy that *we* still have today wasn't written until the 1st century CE, perhaps around 40 CE. In that 300-year gap most of the foundational works of the school's philosophy were written; though we have some partial works, a good deal of quotation, and quite a few excerpts written during this period, to a great extent we are forced to rely on summaries of school doctrines and criticisms directed against them if we want to understand the content and methods of the school for this period. Reconstructing Stoic philosophy from such fragmentary and diverse materials is inevitably a complicated academic enterprise, drawing on advanced historical, linguistic, and philosophical skills. And just

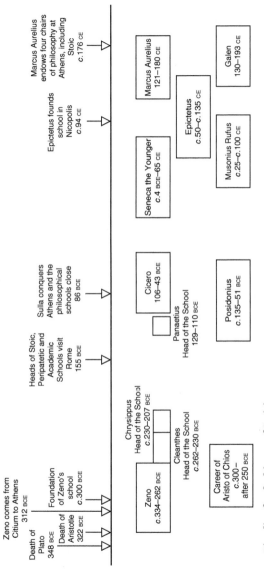

1. Timeline for the history of Stoicism

as inevitably, the topic is full of controversy and scholarly debate—in this it is no different from any other field of historical research. On many issues there is now a fairly broad and stable consensus, and specialists have done a reasonable job of making it available to a wider audience.

But the key point is that we have nothing like the direct voice of ancient Stoic thinkers until we come to the Roman Seneca (about whom I will say more in due course), the Greek teacher Epictetus, and the emperor Marcus Aurelius.

For comparison, think of Platonic philosophy. Though many periods in the history of Platonism are just as badly documented as Stoicism, we also have all of Plato's authentic dialogues, the works from which the school's doctrines grew. Consider Aristotle too, a great many of whose works are lost to us, both popular dialogues and more technical treatises that resembled the ones that we still have. Even with this loss, we have a massive corpus of Aristotle's carefully worked out analytical writing, the works which formed (and still do form) the basis for the enduring Aristotelian tradition in philosophy. It's even better with the late Platonist philosopher Plotinus. Not only do we have all of his treatises (the *Enneads*), but we have detailed information about how the works were composed and how the corpus was put together by his student and editor Porphyry. When we want to understand Platonism, Aristotelianism, or Plotinian Neoplatonism, we can at least read the relevant works by Plato, Aristotle, and Plotinus.

We can't do that for Stoicism. The demanding task of figuring out what earlier Stoics thought and why they thought it is frustratingly indirect. What we can access directly are the works of much later writers, Seneca, Epictetus, and Marcus Aurelius. The fact that they are such vivid, moving, and persuasive writers makes it even harder to see exactly what the earlier school was like. Not only that, but for most modern readers what matters most are the books they can read directly. We are inspired by reading Plato's *Apology* and *Republic*, gripped by the gnarly charm of Aristotle's *Metaphysics* and the calm grandeur of his *Nicomachean Ethics*, alternately frustrated and swept away by Plotinus' vision of an intelligible universe. We simply can't do that with their counterparts in the Stoic school. Scholarly reconstruction just isn't the same thing and inevitably the vigorous prose of Epictetus and Marcus has been dominant in shaping the image of Stoicism in the modern world.

It's time for a quick overview of the school's major figures and a sense of how they fit together historically. The founder of the school was Zeno, a man who immigrated to Athens in the late 4th century BCE from his native city of Citium on the island of Cyprus. Whether he moved to Athens specifically to take up philosophy isn't certain, but once he was there he immediately fell under the sway of the Cynic philosopher Crates (also an immigrant to Athens) whom he regarded as a kind of modern-day Socrates (who had been tried and executed two generations earlier). Over the course of his long life in Athens, Zeno lectured, attracted many students, and became something of a phenomenon; Athens celebrated him with a statue and a formal decree when he died. He also wrote quite a few books on a wide range of philosophical topics (Diogenes Laërtius *Lives of the Philosophers* 7.4)—something that Socrates had never done—books which reflected his active engagement with many other philosophers and schools. Zeno's students, the first generation of Stoics, were a varied group and they disagreed with each other significantly about their teacher's legacy. Some, such as Sphaerus and Persaeus, were interested in political applications of philosophy, as Plato and the Pythagoreans had been in the past; even Aristotle had taught political leaders, although he wasn't himself tempted by direct involvement in political life.

Two of Zeno's students in particular represented importantly different interpretations of Stoic philosophy. Aristo, from the

Aegean island of Chios, argued that physical theory (including what we would call metaphysics) and logic were unproductive intellectual indulgences. Opposing him was Cleanthes, who emphasized natural philosophy (physics) and theology as well as ethics and logical theory. The difference between the two foreshadows important later tensions in the school. On one side you have a Large Stoicism, inclusive of all kinds of intellectual activity, arguing that the ultimately ethical goal of philosophy required knowledge across the entire range of topics of intellectual enquiry; this is the line taken by Cleanthes. On the other side you have Minimal Stoicism, the line taken by Aristo; like the Cynics, he focused exclusively on ethics: the practical application of human reason to the job of making one's life better. Both branches of the school agreed that the ethical ideal could be achieved by 'following nature', but they disagreed profoundly about what is involved in that pursuit.

It's tempting to romanticize the debate between these two approaches, and no doubt there were lively disagreements, even a power struggle. But in the end Cleanthes became the second head of the school, entrenching Large Stoicism as the standard for a long time to come. Under his leadership, and that of his brilliant successor, Chrysippus, from the remote town of Soli in Asia Minor, the school became encyclopedic in its breadth. Chrysippus developed logic into a major preoccupation of the school, revised and enhanced the metaphysical foundations of Stoic cosmology and natural philosophy, and took a particularly stringent line in ethics, all the while working towards an ideal of full integration across all the branches and subdivisions of Stoic thought. Chrysippus' students and their followers dominated the school's approach for over a hundred years, but by the middle of the 2nd century BCE a variety of influences (including powerful criticism from the Academy and the Peripatos, the schools of Plato and Aristotle, respectively) led to a change in the school's approach. This confrontation with Platonic and Aristotelian criticism is symbolized by the debates during a joint visit to Rome in 155 BCE by the leaders of all three schools—by which some Roman politicians were scandalized. Subsequently Panaetius, from the island of Rhodes, and even more so his student Posidonius from Syria, re-engaged with the philosophy of Plato and also that of Aristotle, reducing the school's preoccupation with Chrysippus' legacy, and revitalizing it by adopting and adapting insights from Platonic and Aristotelian philosophy.

Meanwhile, Minimal Stoicism hadn't disappeared completely. It carried on somewhat below the radar, often presenting itself as a form of Cynic thought, resurfacing again clearly in the 1st century CE. In the meantime, though, the official school based in Athens went through a crisis. Like all of the original Athenian schools, Stoicism was massively disrupted by war and politics. The city was conquered and sacked by the Romans under the general Sulla in 86 BCE; though details are unclear, it seems that the schools essentially ceased to function in Athens for quite some time, perhaps not reviving significantly until the 2nd century CE, when Marcus Aurelius re-founded them with endowed chairs of philosophy for each of the four schools (Academic, Peripatetic, Epicurean, Stoic). In the aftermath of the effective closing of the schools, Stoicism became a more decentralized phenomenon. There had already been Stoic schools in Rhodes and elsewhere during the Hellenistic period, but with the decline of the Athenian operation, Stoic schools and individual Stoic philosophers pop up all around the Mediterranean basin: in Rhodes, of course, in Alexandria, and in Rome itself as well as in lesser centres.

Further indication of the fragmentation of the Stoic tradition comes from the reference by a later author (Athenaeus 5.2) to three branches of the school, named for Diogenes, Antipater, and Panaetius, three leading thinkers of the 2nd century BCE. In this pluralistic environment it is not surprising to find profound Stoic influence on the Etruscan philosopher (and Roman citizen) Musonius Rufus, on the Jewish intellectual Philo of Alexandria (both of whom wrote in Greek and were active in the 1st century CE), and on others who shaped philosophical activity at Rome in the early imperial period. Seneca, for example, was never a formal teacher or head of a school, but he remains one of the most prolific Stoic authors we know about. At about the same time we hear of an Egyptian priest-scribe, Chaeremon, who came to Rome and taught Stoicism there. Epictetus, who had been a slave at Nero's court, eventually set up his school in the small town of Nicopolis on the eastern shore of the Adriatic Sea. A student of Posidonius, Asclepiodotus caught Seneca's attention (he is mentioned repeatedly in the *Natural Questions*), and in the next century the Stoic teacher Cleomedes wrote a lengthy and polemical astronomical treatise drawing heavily on Posidonius' work. At about the same time in Asia Minor the Stoic teacher Hierocles wrote a range of works on ethics, both technical and popular. As Jonathan Barnes has established, there is also clear evidence of great activity in the area of Stoic logic at about this time. The Stoic Philopator (in the 2nd century CE) developed ideas about determinism and moral responsibility that caught the attention of critics. It is this rich context of decentralized but high-level philosophical activity that provides the context for the discourses of Epictetus that we still possess and that had such profound influence on Marcus Aurelius. In fact, to judge from the critical engagement with Stoicism by several intellectuals in the 2nd century CE (including Platonists, Aristotelians, and the philosophical doctor Galen), Stoic work in all areas of philosophy was a prominent feature of the intellectual scene right up until the time of Alexander of Aphrodisias and Plotinus in the early 3rd century CE.

And then, almost abruptly, the trail goes cold. Although Stoicism continued to be moderately well-known for a bit longer and had considerable indirect influence on a wide range of intellectual trends in later antiquity (including Christian philosophy and theology), we cease to find significant evidence of interaction between active Stoic philosophers and other schools.

The emperor Marcus Aurelius, whose version of Stoicism was our starting point, was educated and wrote in the atmosphere of that final phase of Stoic thought, the later 2nd century CE, following the inspiration of Epictetus from decades before. The versions of Stoicism that inspired Admiral Stockdale and Pierre Hadot are not stand-alone works of genius (though they are certainly works of genius); they emerge from a rich and complex environment of philosophical theorizing, argument, and debate. As we proceed we will have to keep our eyes on both aspects of Stoicism: the inspirational figures that still live and breathe in our contemporary intellectual climate and the full historical context from which these vital, but perhaps not typical, representatives of ancient Stoicism emerged.

Chapter 2
Reading Stoics today: Epictetus, Marcus Aurelius, and even Seneca

For modern readers, Epictetus and Marcus Aurelius provide the foundation for our understanding of Stoicism. Yet looked at from a historian's perspective, they are hardly typical representatives of the school. The emperor was not a professional philosopher and sometimes expresses views that conflict with what we know about the school from other sources. Some scholars even question whether it is right to count him as a Stoic at all; after all, he credits philosophers from other schools with inspiring his thought and even refers to Stoics in the third person (Stoics are 'they' not 'we'). Epictetus was certainly a professional Stoic—he ran a school where he lectured on the works of Chrysippus and taught his students how to interpret several of the great Stoics of previous generations. But his intellectual context was remote from that of the philosophers who founded the school and developed its doctrines; he worked centuries later and had his intellectual formation at Rome as a slave and freedman, influenced by, among others, Musonius Rufus. The Roman imperial court was presumably not the richest philosophical environment to live in (Epictetus' master was one of Nero's senior civil servants, the Greek Epaphroditus) and in later years he was driven out of Rome by another emperor and set up his own philosophical school in Nicopolis, a town across the Adriatic Sea from Italy on the road to Greece and the East. Though Rome had become a focus for philosophical activity in the 1st century CE, Nicopolis was not.

How this peculiar career path affected his philosophy is hard to imagine, but it could hardly be more different from the intensely philosophical and professional environment in Hellenistic Athens, where the founders and early leaders of the school debated, researched, and lectured in close proximity with leading intellects from other schools. No wonder, then, that so many of Epictetus' discourses address the non-specialist, the non-philosopher even. It's also no wonder that he himself wrote no treatises, whether technical or popular; the discourses he left are in fact a record of his oral teaching kept and published by one of his loyal students, Arrian of Nicomedia in Bithynia, a Roman citizen and politician (consul 132 CE, senator, provincial governor) as well as an intellectual of some distinction writing in Greek.

Prima facie, then, these are not the sources we would ideally look for in trying to understand ancient Stoicism. We moderns have turned to them for two reasons, both readily understandable. First, except for Seneca (about whom more later) theirs are the earliest, in fact almost the only, complete works we have from the ancient Stoics. Even if we wanted to start from the works of the founders, Zeno of Citium and Chrysippus of Soli, we can't; they are all lost. Second, both Epictetus and Marcus are atypical in the way they wrote and the kind of audience they chose to address, atypical in ways that make them more effective authors, perhaps, but not necessarily the best reflections of the traditional doctrines of the school. For Epictetus the point is readily seen: the discourses are a record of the lectures he delivered to laymen and aspiring philosophers, and not to those whose aim was to master the finer points of Zeno's cosmology, Chrysippus' metaphysics, or Posidonius' theory of matter and causation. As to Marcus, he often puts himself in the very position many of us find ourselves in. Not being philosophers, we too might turn to philosophy as a source of perspective, reflection, and guidance; his book is a kind of philosophical diary, intensely personal and idiosyncratic. For Marcus, Stoic philosophy is often held at arm's length, as it is by many of us.

But how did it happen that Epictetus' and Marcus' works have survived intact, more or less, and have shaped so much of our understanding of Stoicism? This is a story that comes in two parts. The part that tells us most about where we are today is a bit of modern intellectual history, the account of how Epictetus and Marcus (along with Seneca) were discovered (or rediscovered) in the Renaissance and came to be printed, distributed, translated, and popularized all over Europe. It's a story that concludes with today's plethora of paperback translations of both authors, their inclusion on Great Books reading lists, and wide influence all around the world. In this story, Epictetus and Marcus come across as near equals, twin beacons of an ancient school of thought just different enough from each other to attract different character types with comparable energy. But the first part of the story is different; it is the account of how these authors survived late antiquity and the middle ages securely enough, sufficiently intact, that they were available to inspire the new thinkers of the Renaissance and so to become an influential part of the modern world.

In this context Epictetus and Marcus suffer fates that could not be more different. Epictetus had become an important figure already in the 2nd century CE, emulated by many and exercising influence over the great and powerful in Roman society—not least the emperor Marcus himself. In later centuries he was adopted by Platonists, the uncontested winners of the contest for pagan philosophical survival in late antiquity, and so assured himself of impact in the centuries to come. Marcus, though, suffered a very different fate. His personal notebook, or philosophical diary, seems to have been unknown or unappreciated for centuries, barely surviving—perhaps, as Pierre Hadot suggests, only because his family kept it safe. Eventually it was rediscovered, virtually by accident, by a leader of the medieval Orthodox church—so that it was only in the 10th century CE that the survival of the book was at all assured. From there the story of its continued survival and wider influence is a bit more straightforward. According to Ada

Palmer, the first known modern reference to Marcus' work was in 1517; but it is only in the 17th century that Marcus' book took its place alongside Epictetus and Seneca, becoming an important part of modern intellectual history and shaping our conception of ancient Stoicism in a decisive way. (The first edition of Marcus in Greek had been published in 1559, over a hundred years after Epictetus' work had become available in a Latin translation.)

The fact that Epictetus and Marcus have exercised disproportionate influence on the popular understanding of Stoicism has a great deal to do with their heavy concentration on ethical themes. In late antiquity and the middle ages, and consequently also in the early modern period, physics and metaphysics were dominated by the twin giants of ancient thought, Plato and Aristotle. Ancient works on physics by Stoics, then, tended to disappear in the middle ages, their content surviving only very indirectly in so far as it was absorbed into the synthesis of later Platonism and referred to by commentators on Aristotle. When the Platonist-Aristotelian synthesis of the middle ages was decisively challenged by a revival of empirical science in the early modern period, the ancient theory that could inspire an alternative approach was atomism rather than Stoicism (which shared a great deal with Platonic and Aristotelian physics, as we will see later). It was, then, in ethics and to some extent in social and political theory that Stoicism came to play an important role as an influence on the development of modern thought. One important factor here is that the three main Stoic authors (Seneca, Epictetus, and Marcus) were active in the period that was foundational for the early Christian church. (Indeed, the legend of Seneca's correspondence with St Paul persisted remarkably long into the modern world, being exploded eventually by Erasmus.) Various features of their ethical thinking made Stoicism a foil for debate among Christian thinkers, while other features, such as the theory of the passions and moral weakness, became an inspiration (not always acknowledged) for ascetic versions of Christian faith. As the focus of Christian historiography and ecclesiology shifted to Greek sources (which were indeed the most important for the development of the early church), Greek pagan texts, such as Marcus and Epictetus, took on a special salience, especially in Protestant countries. By the late 19th century we are not surprised to see that Marcus Aurelius has become a source of spiritual influence among Christians of a progressive bent, especially in Victorian Britain, whose imperial ambitions found in the emperor parallels to their own situation, and that Protestant intellectuals, such as Adolf Bonhöffer, devoted enormous energy to the study of Epictetus. By the early 20th century, then, Epictetus and Marcus had emerged as holding a special place in European intellectual life.

The other ancient Stoic whose writings have survived more or less intact ought, from a certain point of view, to be even more important than Epictetus and Marcus. The Roman author and politician Lucius Annaeus Seneca is, in fact, the earliest of the Stoic authors whose works have survived in nearly complete form from antiquity; he wrote in the 1st century CE (he lived from around 4 BCE to 65 CE), overlapping in his mature years with the young Epictetus; although both were part of Nero's imperial court there is no evidence that Seneca knew Epictetus; and any sign that Epictetus or Marcus knew Seneca or his work is circumstantial at best. Yet Seneca's Stoic works are far more extensive than those of the other two taken together and they cover a wider range of philosophical themes. Hence they were of particular importance to Renaissance intellectuals, and in particular to Justus Lipsius, the Dutch scholar who published the first genuinely scholarly studies of ancient Stoicism in the last decade of the 16th century and the first decade of the 17th. Unlike Marcus, Seneca was a professed Stoic who unhesitatingly identified with the school. Unlike Epictetus, he was not a teacher and never lectured on Stoicism in a professional way; and also unlike Epictetus he wrote copiously in several different genres. His works were all written in Latin, rather than Greek, which was the language used by the vast majority of philosophers in the ancient world, including all the early Stoics, Epictetus, and Marcus. Even other Roman contemporaries of Seneca who dealt with Stoic themes (such as Musonius Rufus and Cornutus) wrote their philosophical works in Greek. In part because he wrote in Latin—and also because he was alleged to have been a Christian sympathizer who corresponded with St Paul—his works survived remarkably well in the Latin tradition of western Europe. There are surviving works on ethics, for the most part, but also on physics and theology and even snippets on logic—though, like Epictetus, Seneca tended to think that his contemporaries put too much emphasis on logic, so that most of what he says about logic is in a critical vein.

With such a large corpus of Seneca's works on Stoicism—works whose influence survived through the middle ages to the 18th century, covering a range of themes—why is Seneca not a more important figure in our contemporary popular understanding of Stoicism? How did the Stoic whose legacy was of such basic importance in the later middle ages and the Renaissance come to take a back seat in general culture?

This question is even more puzzling when you look at the trajectory of Seneca's influence. As a Latin author and one who was influential for his prose style as well as for the content of his works, he was known almost continuously through the middle ages, and in the Renaissance he was the first Stoic author 'rediscovered'. Until Greek authors became available he had been the main touchstone for revival of interest in Stoicism and (along with Cicero, the Academic whose dialogues in Latin, written in the 50s and 40s BCE, provided a great deal of information about the school) was a crucially important source of information about Stoicism. Seneca's influence in many quarters was greatly increased owing to his association with the Roman empire. In times and places where the Romans were thought of as a model of or inspiration for culture and politics in the modern world, Seneca's works took on a special importance. Though he could not easily be associated with republican virtues, as could Cicero, he could be portrayed as part of the resistance to the tyrannical monarch Nero (even though he was in fact a key member of his regime for many years). The so-called 'Stoic opposition' to the emperor's overreach was loosely associated with Seneca (which may have been why Nero eventually forced him to commit suicide), and in his philosophical writings Seneca turned Cato the Younger, political hero of the late republic, into a philosophical hero as well: a Roman version of the Stoic sage. The result is that when the Roman republic was looked to as a source of political ideas Seneca and his Stoicism took on exceptional interest.

Seneca's influence was always stronger in some parts of Europe than others; he was of great interest to Reformation theologians such as Erasmus and Calvin, and he was especially popular in France, Italy, and his native Spain (Seneca was born in the ancient Roman colony of Corduba, modern Córdoba). Nevertheless, he is hardly the beacon for the revival of Stoicism in the modern world that Epictetus and Marcus have become. The reasons for this are complex, and a large part of the story seems to turn on the fact that his works are in Latin—not the prestige language of philosophy in the ancient world and consequently less central in the reception of ancient philosophy since the 19th century. Other considerations are the fact that he was an exceptionally versatile author in areas outside philosophy, writing in many genres of poetry and prose. An accomplished and flashy stylist, he was a literary lion in his own day, not the sort of figure that we tend to associate with serious philosophical reflection. Even worse, he was a politician, and not just a politician but a privileged adviser to the emperor Nero, a position which made him exceptionally wealthy and deeply compromised, especially after Nero's fall from popularity. Hence a reputation for glib hypocrisy has tended to mar his legacy (it's hard to imagine anything worse for a philosopher's credibility, especially one who wrote so much on ethics) and this, as much as anything else, has tended to dampen modern enthusiasm for his work and to limit his influence in popular culture. Specialists, not least Ilsetraut Hadot and Michel Foucault (especially in *The Care of the Self* and in *The Hermeneutics of the Subject*), have explored Seneca's influence on ancient practices of moral improvement and moral education, but in the last 150 years he has not rivalled Marcus and Epictetus in his impact on the popular understanding of Stoicism.

Despite all of that, Seneca's works remain some of our best sources of insight into ancient Stoic thought. When we turn our attention to the history of the ancient school itself, in contrast to the image of it in modern thought, we will (like Lipsius) find ourselves drawing on his works quite often. But here we are considering instead the shape of our modern understanding of Stoic thought and its meaning for the contemporary world. And that is where his impact has been less than one might have expected. It would be a rewarding thought experiment to imagine how different the contemporary image of Stoicism might be if he did take his place alongside the ex-slave and the emperor. One difference would certainly be in our appreciation for the significance of physics and natural philosophy—Seneca, after all, wrote a lengthy work entitled *Natural Questions*, one of his most important and substantial works. We might also think of Stoicism as being a little less gloomy and sober-sided than we do—Seneca was the author of a wickedly funny lampoon of the Roman emperor Claudius, imagining that he was 'pumpkinified' rather than deified at his death. Without a doubt we would think of Stoicism as much more engaged with theoretical reflection on social and political philosophy rather than mere personal improvement—Seneca's *On Benefits* and *On Clemency* are among the more significant works of social and political thought to survive from antiquity. Though Seneca doesn't embrace logical sophistication for its own sake any more than Epictetus does, he would certainly counterbalance the sense that we get from Marcus that technical expertise in logic and metaphysics is dispensable for the true Stoic. In general, where Marcus encourages the idea, adopted enthusiastically by Pierre Hadot, that the fundamental message of Stoicism, a moral creed, is somehow independent of physics and seriously argued theoretical enquiry, Seneca does just the opposite. Even more than

Epictetus, Seneca makes it clear that philosophical theorizing and debate, along with engaged problem solving, are essential to the ultimate goal of making human life better. As we turn to a consideration of the earlier history of the school, this integrated conception of Stoic philosophy will be revealed as a key feature of the school's message.

Chapter 3
The origins of the school: Stoicism and Plato

The earliest Stoics shared a great deal with Plato and his followers, not least the fact that they put Socrates on a pedestal as a kind of philosophical hero (and so did the Cynics, who also had a powerful influence over the Stoics). As we will see, the Stoics were also in strong agreement with Plato—or, rather, his spokesman the Pythagorean 'Timaeus', whose theory of the universe is laid out in the dialogue named for him. In the *Timaeus* we are told that the cosmos is a single, living organism, created by a benevolent god (the Craftsman or Demiurge) who wants there to be as much goodness and order as possible in the world. This world is organized to a great extent for the benefit of its most privileged inhabitants, rational mortal animals—human beings. Like Xenophon, another writer of Socratic dialogues whose works appealed to the founder Zeno, Plato thought that the effective organization of the human body and the fact that the world apparently exists to serve our needs (if only we are wise enough to use it well) were clear signs that a benevolent and providential divinity established our world and continues to run it in the most orderly and helpful way possible.

One might well ask, then, why the early Stoics didn't just join the school Plato founded, the Academy. The question becomes more pressing when we take account of the fact that Zeno actually studied with the fourth leader of the Academy, a philosopher named Polemo. Plato's school was a relatively liberal operation, intellectually—though it is certainly possible that Aristotle failed to get the headship after Plato died owing to his philosophical disagreements with other leading Platonists, in particular Speusippus (Plato's nephew who in the end took over the school). In very late antiquity the Platonist philosopher Simplicius saw enough common ground with Stoicism that he devoted great effort to writing a commentary on the *Handbook* of Epictetus. So what *was* the problem?

In a word, metaphysics. Plato's most distinctive doctrine was his theory of Forms. Although the exact formulation of the theory varied over the course of his career, Plato is still most strongly associated with the idea that there are incorporeal Forms corresponding to things in the physical realm, each one a unique and unchanging reality, distinct from and the cause of the physical particulars that 'participate' in them. The Athenian statesman Aristides is just; the laws of a good city are just; but these things are just because they *participate* in Justice—a Form which is perfect and never changes, whereas the politician Aristides could conceivably become a crook later in life, and some cities presumably have laws that are only approximately and unreliably just. Helen of Troy is beautiful, as is a brilliant painting or a perfect sunset. But they are beautiful because they *participate* in Beauty, a Form which, unlike Helen, the painting, and the sunset, will never fade.

Forms did a lot of work in Plato's metaphysics, and even today there is a lively debate about the details of his theory. Forms give meaning to words; without them Plato worried that discourse would be impossible (*Parmenides* 135). They are the causes *par excellence* of things and their properties (*Phaedo* 99–107). And they are the proper objects of knowledge (*Republic* 476–480). The physical particulars that we see all around us cannot be known because they aren't stable enough and precise enough to be the object of a cognitive state that is itself perfect and secure. To do all of this work, Forms had to be somehow distinct from the particulars they cause, and this distinctness came to be labelled 'separation'. There is still a wide-ranging debate about what separation actually meant to Plato, but Aristotle, at least, saw it (along with the insufficiently explained notion of 'participation') as a fatal weakness in Platonic theory.

So too did the Stoics. In their view, Platonic Forms cannot be distinct and separate substances that cause physical particulars to be what they are. They were introduced by Plato, according to the Stoics, to account for the concepts or thoughts that humans have—and that's all they really are: human thoughts elevated artificially to a special metaphysical status to which they have no rightful claim—and to explain how our language works, how it is that we can use general terms reliably in our discourse with others. But nothing more than that is justified. They emphatically should not be considered to be the causes of anything, since, as the Stoics saw things, incorporeal entities cannot act or be acted upon at all—though such things may be an important part of our account of the world, they have no causal efficacy whatsoever.

As we will see shortly, the Stoics replaced Platonic metaphysics with a fundamentally new theory. Without a commitment to Forms of some kind one could hardly be a Platonist, and this may have been the issue that drove even Aristotle out of the Platonist world he had been educated in. As he famously said, the advocates of the Forms may be friends, but the truth comes first (*Nicomachean Ethics* 1096a12–16). Zeno's relationship with Platonists was never as intimate as Aristotle's was, and his metaphysical revisionism was even more radical. He could share with Plato his hero worship of Socrates; his conviction that virtue is the key to happiness (and that there are four basic forms of virtue); his idea that the world is a divinely created order with a special place for humans in it; and his dedication to the idea that knowledge is a cognitive state of the highest perfection, not admitting of doubt, variance, or revision. But he could not accept Forms. And so (despite the feeble efforts by the renegade Academic Antiochus of Ascalon some centuries later, in the 1st century BCE) Stoicism had to become its own separate philosophy.

A brilliant French philosopher-scholar, the late Jacques Brunschwig, identified the philosophical crux that seems to have inspired Zeno to break away from Platonic metaphysics in the way he did. A fascinating passage (245e–249d) in one of Plato's later dialogues, the *Sophist*, provided Zeno with the way of handling the disagreement about incorporeal Forms which set him on his own path in metaphysics. (See Box 2 for key selections from this

Stoicism

Box 2 Plato's *Sophist*

—In fact, because they disagree with each other about being, it seems that there is among them a virtual battle between the Gods and Giants.

—What do you mean?

—One side pulls everything down from the heavens, that is, the invisible realm, to the earth—they actually grasp rocks and trees with their bare hands. And when they get a hold on everything of the sort, they assert that only things that admit of touch and contact *are*, stipulating that body and being are the same thing. And if someone says that anything else that's incorporeal *is* they hold him in utter contempt and refuse to listen to anything else that he says.

—You've described truly frightening people, certainly. I've already met quite a few of them.

—Therefore, those who take the other side in the debate are very careful in the way they fight them off, taking their stand somewhere up in the invisible realm and insisting forcefully that true being is certain intelligible and incorporeal forms.... (246a–b)

—So let's ask them again. For if they are willing to concede
that even a small portion of the things that *are* is incorporeal,
that's enough. They will have to explain what turns out to be
common both to these things and to corporeal things, that is,
what it is that they refer to when they claim that both kinds of
things *are*. And maybe they will be stumped by that. And if that
is their experience, consider whether they would be prepared to
accept a suggestion from us and agree that being is something
like this.

—Like what? Come on, tell me and then maybe we'll know.

—Well, I'm suggesting that something which has any kind of
capacity at all, whether it's naturally able to act on something
else or to be acted on by something else (no matter how small
it itself is or how trivial the thing that acts on it is, and even if it
does so only once)—everything of this sort genuinely *is*. I propose
that we should take this as a definition: things which *are* are
nothing but a capacity. (247c–e)

passage.) From there he developed an entire philosophical system
that would first compete successfully with Platonic metaphysics
and then, centuries later, ultimately lose the debate initiated in
that dialogue.

The Giants in Plato's just-so story (whom we shall meet again in
the pages to come) 'pull everything down from the heavens, that
is, the invisible realm, to the earth' and 'assert that only things
that admit of touch and contact *are*, stipulating that body and
being are the same thing'. A more modest version of their stance
is given a bit later:

> something which has any kind of capacity at all, whether it's
> naturally able to act on something else or to be acted on by
> something else (no matter how small it itself is or how trivial the

thing that acts on it is, and even if it does so only once)—everything of this sort genuinely *is*.

Stoics were by no means unsophisticated in their response to Plato, but in the end Zeno took the view that anything that *is* must have the capacity to have an effect on other things or to be affected by something else, and that only a body had such capacities (Cicero, *Academica* 1.39). In contrast, anything non-bodily has no such capacity (Sextus Empiricus, *adversus Mathematicos* 8.263). This materialism was maintained by Stoics right through to the end of the school's history (unless Marcus Aurelius harboured some doubts, as I will suggest in Chapter 4).

While it may seem quite a familiar and plausible idea that only something corporeal can act or be acted upon, it depended on a bold new conception of causation that was at odds with the ideas of Plato and Aristotle and their followers. It also came at a fairly high cost, at least from a Platonic point of view. It meant, for example, that the soul (which clearly acts on the body and is acted upon by it) must be material, even though it is invisible and intangible. Qualities and other features of bodies must also be bodily, since they interact causally with physical things; hence the virtues too, so exalted metaphysically in Plato's theory of Forms, turn out to be conditions of the material soul. Aristides doesn't *participate* in the Form of Justice; his justice consists in particular modifications of his corporeal soul. Even God must be bodily, and so the Platonic idea that bodily things are necessarily perishable had to be confronted. Nevertheless, some things, such as time and spatial extension (both occupied and empty) proved to be stubbornly non-bodily. These 'incorporeals', as the Stoics called them, could have no causal power, even though they are needed to give an account of the physical world. Consequently the Stoics had to develop a metaphysical status for such things which acknowledged their 'reality' without treating them as bodies. And that meant that a higher category was needed to encompass both the incorporeal and the corporeal beings—and so they posited the notorious 'somethings' to do the job, a move to which many critics took serious exception. 'Being' was no longer the highest genus in the kind of hierarchical metaphysical categorization so beloved of Platonists and even Aristotelians in later antiquity.

But once this radically new metaphysics was in place it provided Stoics with a tool for tackling other problems that arose. Plato held that Forms somehow gave meaning to our words and our thoughts, and enabled us to communicate; for you to understand what I mean when I say 'horse' requires that we both have access to the common Form of horse, which is what gives reliable meaning to my words whether spoken aloud or silently thought. Without Forms how could the Stoics account for the meaning and content of our discourse? The answer came in the form of a new sort of incorporeal, the 'sayable' (*lekton*), which doesn't exist in the strong sense of *being* but which has a dependent sort of reality. My thoughts and utterances all have meaningful content owing to the presence of such sayables. Our efforts at communication will succeed if my words (themselves physical modifications of the air) cause you to have the same thoughts that I had when I uttered them. The words do so by causing your soul to be modified in such a way that the same sayable content attaches to your psychological states as was present to my soul when I spoke.

One other thing which Forms did in Platonic theory, at least on some interpretations, was to provide a metaphysical status for universals. If all the particulars of some kind are the same as other members of that kind—everything truly called a horse is the same, in so far as it is a horse—this universal fact must have a basis in reality. For Platonists that basis is the Form rather than a mere psychological concept that we might just happen to share. But as we have seen, Stoics reject this way of accounting for universals when they say that Forms just are our thoughts (*ennoēmata*, a term that is often and reasonably translated as 'concepts'). These concepts are not real beings, in Stoic theory, though they were meant to stand in the place of Forms in an account of universals.

What that meant, in effect, is that universals were not underpinned by stable real beings but are just the result in our minds of the relatively uniform experience we have of the objects in the world, experience that we ultimately acquire by means of sense perception. The Stoics adopted a version of what would later be termed 'nominalism', as did Aristotle and other schools (such as the Epicureans) who denied the independent existence of Forms as the referent of universal terms.

The Stoics, then, were Giants in Plato's sense, reducing everything real (in the strongest sense) to bodies. The impact of this metaphysical revolution was substantial; it distinguished Stoicism from other schools in most areas of philosophical activity and seems to have been the foundation of their distinctness. In other areas, such as epistemology and ethics (both theory and practice), Stoics also had distinctive views, not all of which originated in their metaphysical commitments. But for an account of what fundamentally made the Stoics into a separate school with their own agenda in the ancient world we need look no further.

Although metaphysics was the most important factor driving Stoics to set themselves up as a distinct school, it was not a distinct field, as such, within Stoic philosophy, which formally recognized physics, ethics, and logic. In the following chapters we will look at the principal Stoic commitments and theories in each of these areas; we won't always have room for a full account of the deep motivations behind the doctrines, unfortunately, but the Further reading section will provide pointers to more specialized literature that deals with that aspect of Stoicism in greater depth.

If Stoicism doesn't consist simply of ethics and practical advice for a happy life, what is it really? The answer lies in what our ancient sources tell us about their conception of philosophy. From the beginning, the ancient Stoics divided philosophy as they understood it into three parts: logic, physics, and ethics. In doing so they were following the suggestion of an early Platonist,

Xenocrates (396–314 BCE, the third head of the Academy), but the idea that philosophy (or philosophical discourse—both ways of making the point are attested) consisted of those three subjects was far from uncontroversial. Plato himself never formally carved philosophy up into parts; Aristotle's followers and perhaps Aristotle himself thought of logic as a tool that one used in doing philosophy rather than as a part of it (though at *Topics* 1.14, 105b19–29, Aristotle seems more sympathetic to Xenocrates' tripartition). Epicurus too treated the study of argument and investigative methods as distinct and instrumental—he called it 'canonic' or the study of criteria. For Aristotle there was a basic distinction between practical and theoretical philosophy, with ethics falling into the practical branch (along with politics and rhetoric) and physics, metaphysics, and the mathematical sciences falling into the theoretical (the various theoretical sciences being distinguished by the nature of the objects they study). So when the Stoics adopted the division into logic, physics, and ethics it wasn't the sort of thing they could take for granted.

Logic itself was far more than what we mean by logic today; it included more than analysis of valid forms of inference, covering everything connected to the study of *logos* (language or discourse): rhetoric, philosophy of language, and linguistics. Physics covered theories about the nature of matter, the origins and development of the cosmos, astronomy, the nature of the gods, ecology, and much more. Ethics studied everything about the good human life, and so political philosophy was as much a part of it as the analysis of personal happiness that focused on conceptions of the goal of life (the *telos*) and the nature of value. It's not clear where the Stoics thought disciplines like mathematics really belonged, and many branches of modern philosophy also wind up straddling the boundaries of the Stoic division: philosophy of mind, epistemology, and metaphysics are the clearest examples; but philosophy of science and aesthetics are also relevant to more than one branch of Stoic philosophy.

For the Stoics, then, philosophy was a lot more than ethics, care of the soul, and prescriptions for a way of life. For most Stoics, all three parts of philosophy were essential; the exceptions to this were few, chiefly Aristo of Chios, the student of Zeno who claimed that ethics was not just the essential heart of philosophy but also the only part needed; he thought that logic in particular was a wasteful intellectual self-indulgence. But even the Stoics who agreed on the need for all three parts did not agree on the relationships among them. Various analogies capture their different views. When they compared philosophy to a living animal there were different views. For some, logic is like the bones and sinews; ethics is like the fleshy parts; and physics is like the soul. But for the great Posidonius, ethics is like the soul and physics like the flesh and blood. Other Stoics compared philosophy to an egg, with logic being the shell, ethics the egg-white (which protects and nourishes the embryonic chick), and physics being the yolk, where the embryo will grow and become the new animal.

Some of these comparisons suggest that physics is the ultimate point of philosophy, with ethics nourishing it (the egg-white) or enabling its function (as flesh makes it possible for the soul to perform its activities) and logic as some sort of protection from external threat (the egg-shell) or structural principle supporting the entire edifice of reason. Posidonius, however, clearly treated ethics as the ultimate point of philosophy. But there were other comparisons besides a living animal and an egg, and they expressed different views on how philosophy is structured. If philosophy is like an agricultural field then its fence or wall is logic, again protecting it from external threats; and physics is the land or the trees; while the fruit itself is ethics—here too ethics seem to play the role of ultimate end. Other Stoics compared philosophy to a well-organized city, run on rational principles and protected by a wall; perhaps logic is the wall, but rational principles are to be found everywhere in such a city.

Clearly not all Stoics agreed on whether ethics or physics was the ultimate point of philosophy. Neither did they agree on how to teach the various parts of philosophy, a question that reflects on the relative importance and accessibility of the parts. Some, including Zeno, said that the order should be logic, physics, ethics; others put ethics first or second instead of last. While Posidonius wanted the teaching to start with physics, Chrysippus wanted the order to be logic, ethics, physics, with theology in the culminating position within physics. Other Stoics, perhaps those we might think of as having a more sensible view, recognized that there was an inextricable mixture of the parts of philosophy and so they didn't even try to separate them from each other in teaching.

Given the widespread variation on this issue within the school we should perhaps not worry too much about what Stoicism as such has to say about which part of philosophy is most important. With the exception of Aristo and a few others, Stoics agreed that all three parts had an important role to play, and it would be a mistake to claim that Stoic philosophy is *really* all about certain ethical and spiritual practices, with doctrine in physics and logic playing a more or less extrinsic role. Certainly there were later Stoics, such as Seneca and Epictetus, who objected vigorously to overemphasizing the role of logic and dialectic (formal argumentation), but that is a far cry from holding that logic isn't an important component of philosophy. Intellectual practices that stand outside philosophy and serve it were recognized by Posidonius (at least according to Seneca in *Letter* 88)—things like geometry and optics, for example. No Stoic put logic or physics in that kind of subordinate position in relation to ethics.

Even Epictetus, who promoted a distinct way of organizing philosophical teaching into three 'topics' (see *Discourses* 3.2), recognized that logic was included in philosophy proper. His 'topics' were (1) management of desire and aversion (to avoid wanting the unattainable); (2) controlling one's inclinations so that one could behave appropriately on all occasions; and (3) dialectical sophistication, to avoid making mistakes in one's reasoning in any of the topics. Even physics cannot be separated from this way of organizing philosophy, though it is clearly in the background. For there is no way of knowing what we can and cannot achieve without a proper study of the natural world and its divine governance (we'll discuss this more in Chapter 4). Similarly, we cannot figure out what behaviour is appropriate for human beings if we don't know what kind of animal we are, as Plato's Socrates had recommended in the *Phaedrus* (230a); and that topic is clearly part of the study of the natural world. Divine governance of an ordered world and the natural sociability of the human species are as much a part of physics as the study of the heavenly bodies or the nature of the four elements. Clearly Epictetus' three topics are a case of the 'mixed' mode of teaching Stoic doctrine mentioned earlier, rather than a significant change in how he saw ethics in relation to the rest of philosophy.

Chapter 4
Physics

One of the main dividing lines in Greek physical theory was the question of the nature of matter (for which Aristotle's term *hulē* became standard). Even before Aristotle formalized the conception of matter in his own brilliantly detailed physical theory, philosophers differed about the topic. Some treated matter as a homogeneous kind of stuff, divisible into particles not subject to further division (that is, they were atomists), while others took a more qualitative approach, rejecting the notion of ultimate atomic particles and the companion notion that there is void separating those particles from each other. Empedocles, for example, held that there are four basic kinds of material stuff (earth, air, fire, and water, though he used a range of different names for them) and no empty space in the universe; he held that each of these stuffs is elemental, not subject to change except for the kind of spatial rearrangement involved when these stuffs mix with each other to produce the complex bodies we observe.

The founders of atomism, Leucippus and Democritus, developed an elaborate theory that claimed to explain the qualitative variety that we observe in terms of the interaction of atoms that do not differ in quality but have different sizes and shapes. In the Hellenistic period this general strategy for explaining the world was inherited and developed further by Epicurus and his followers. The Empedoclean tradition was picked up by Aristotle, who claimed that the cosmos was made up of four simple bodies (earth, air, fire, and water), the main difference from Empedocles' theory being that for Aristotle these bodies are not ultimate and unchangeable. For Aristotle, basic qualities (hot, cold, wet, and dry) underlie these simple bodies, which are not elemental. Air can change into water, water into earth, etc.; and the mutual transformation of these qualitatively defined bodies is one of the main features of his theory of the natural world, replacing the simpler combination and compounding used by Empedocles and the atomists. His theory of qualitative transformation was a greatly improved version of earlier Presocratic theories that allowed for such changes among different quality-stuffs.

Plato's theory, as developed in the *Timaeus*, also recognized the four basic Empedoclean bodies, but like Aristotle after him he did not think that they are unchangeable. Being composed of irreducible geometrical parts (triangular surfaces that get combined into three-dimensional particles) these basic bodies can for the most part be transformed into one another by a breakdown and rearrangement of the triangles. Thus water, air, and fire admit of mutual transformation while earth, being made of uniquely shaped triangles, is exempt from this cycle of change. Since these forms of matter are in fact explicable in terms of non-qualitative components (the triangles) it is tempting to regard Plato's theory as a kind of mathematical atomism (no doubt owing much to Pythagorean predecessors), but for all practical purposes Plato comes across more as a four-element theorist than as an atomist.

The unique position of earth is a special feature of Plato's theory, and Aristotle too introduces a very significant wrinkle into the tidy four-element theory. Having matched each of the four simple bodies with a characteristic kind of motion (earth and water move linearly towards the centre; air and fire, towards the periphery of the spherical cosmos), Aristotle had to posit a fifth kind of matter for the heavenly bodies, which have a characteristic circular motion. Plato too recognized the special character of the eternal heavenly bodies, and one of the more contested issues in ancient physical theory remained the question of whether the heavens (essentially, the part of the cosmos further out from earth than the moon) are made of different stuff and follow different rules than those that apply here on earth and in its immediate environs.

Against this background, the Stoics fit squarely into the non-atomistic tradition, being definitely committed to the infinite divisibility of matter, the rejection of void, and the fundamental role of four basic forms of matter, earth, air, fire, and water. Unlike Plato and Aristotle, Stoics did not think that they needed to postulate a special kind of stuff for the heavenly bodies or that the eternal heavens operated by different laws. To be sure, fire was often regarded as an element with varying properties, both creative (or 'technical', that is, craftsmanlike) and destructive, and the creative fire is the element responsible for life and motion. This rejection of a separate divine sphere marks another and very important difference between the Stoics and the Aristotelian/ Platonic traditions. Stoics regarded the universe as a more radical unity, with the divine power that sustains it (something that both Plato and Aristotle believed in, unlike the atomists) not hived off into a distinct metaphysical or superlunary realm but rather infused throughout the entire material world—as it has to be if it is going to have causal impact on the rest of the matter in the universe. We will return to this aspect of Stoic physics later.

For the Stoics, the entire organized world, or cosmos, is made up of these four elements, their mixtures and compounds, all in constant motion. There is no void inside the cosmos (though unlike Aristotle the Stoics did posit emptiness outside the cosmos) and matter in all its forms is infinitely divisible, something they agreed with Aristotle about. However, in contrast to Aristotle the Stoics associated one basic quality with each form of matter (fire is hot, air is cold, earth is dry, and water is wet), rather than two, and all matter tends towards the centre of the spherical cosmos, though of course in varying degrees; this convergence helps to explain the cohesion and unity of the cosmos. Like Plato in the *Timaeus* the Stoics regarded the cosmos as something alive; but while Plato had a separate creator god animate the world by giving it a soul the Stoics show a preference for a radically unified conception of the cosmos. There is a divinity that makes the cosmos alive, but it is material and immanent throughout the cosmos, being called 'Zeus' or 'god' or 'Nature', and identified with the purest form of the element fire.

Aristotle, whose cosmology is in some ways very similar to that of the Stoics, had held that the cosmos was eternal, sustained by a non-physical god 'outside' it, a god that serves as the ultimate and unchanging mover by being an object of admiration and love for the heavenly bodies and, ultimately, everything in the cosmos. The Stoic cosmos is radically unified and its sustaining god is not external; god is the productive, active, or 'creative' feature of the world, penetrating everywhere, ensuring its cohesion and endowing it with a unity that is rational and orderly through and through. The Stoic cosmos is only eternal in a modified sense. Following Empedocles, perhaps, the Stoics reconcile what appear to be the slow-moving changes in the world with the permanence that any divinely grounded entity is supposed to have by positing a cyclical pattern of change. As Empedocles supposed, there is a kind of permanence in any regularly recurring pattern of change, and the Stoics hypothesized their own cosmic cycle—not driven by the competing forces of Love and Strife but guided throughout by the one genuinely permanent agent in their cosmology, Zeus (or Nature), in his guise as pure fire.

According to the Stoic theory (see Figure 2), we are to imagine a starting point for the world, when all that exists is the fiery perfection of god. For some reason known only to god's perfect rationality, creation begins when part of the divine fire condenses into a liquid containing the seed of all future objects and changes. The liquid then undergoes two further transformations. Some of it vaporizes into air and some condenses further into earth. Since pure elemental fire also remains, the evolving cosmos now has all of its basic material components. At this point the guiding principles embedded in fire drive the rest of the developmental process that leads to the world as we know it, with its magnificent variety of beings (minerals which are inert; plants which grow, reproduce, and die; animals which do all of this and also perceive and move themselves; and human beings who share the gift of divine, self-conscious rationality). As perfect as this world may be, it is not wholly stable. The power of fire increases over time in an orderly pattern and one day in the distant future its 'fuel' (derived from the other elements) will be exhausted and the entire cosmos will become a flame (the conflagration), returning once again to its singular starting point; and then the whole process begins

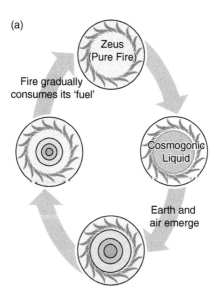

(a)

Zeus
(Pure Fire)

Fire gradually
consumes its 'fuel'

Cosmogonic
Liquid

Earth and
air emerge

All four elements form a cosmos
(including plants, animals, humans, etc.)
governed by immanent fire/reason/Zeus

2. (a) The cosmic cycle.

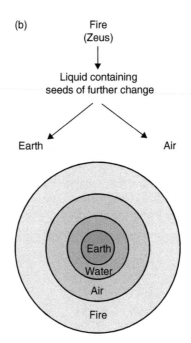

2. (b) **The four forms of matter arrange themselves in concentric circles.**

again, repeating itself forever. (It seems that the repetition of the world cycles is an issue of only theoretical interest to humans, since our lives are confined to one of the cycles. It is clear that the Stoics believed that the recurring cycles are essentially the same, but there seems to have been some disagreement about whether their eternal recurrence involves *exactly* identical objects and events in each recurrent cycle.)

This is the 'big picture' of Stoic cosmology and so far we have focused on its relationship to the main traditions of Greek cosmology and especially on how it relates to Aristotle's and Plato's theories. But Stoic theory was not static and there was a good deal of debate and development over the school's history; there are some aspects of the theory that remain unclear to scholars to this day, owing to the limited and sometimes conflicting evidence we have about the details of the theory. As an example of the debate, consider Panaetius (2nd century BCE), who either doubted or flatly rejected the doctrine of cyclical conflagration, presumably having reasons to opt for a stable universe like Aristotle's; perhaps he was disturbed, as anyone might be, by the lack of any articulable reason why god should initiate the process of cosmogenesis at any given time—or at all. An example of development can be found in the way Chrysippus and later Stoics moved beyond the idea, advanced by Zeno and Cleanthes, that the immanent rational principle guiding the world's changes was a form of fire, and proposed instead that a kind of life-giving breath (*pneuma*, later translated into Latin as *spiritus*) was the animating force in the world. *Pneuma* was a traditional word for breath, but in Stoic hands it became a technical term, one that was put to extensive use in their physical theory. A unique compound of fire and air, *pneuma* was identified as the all-pervasive material stuff that guides the natural world both as a whole and in all of its parts. Warm, elastic air is the locus, then, of life and indeed makes every object what it is. Arguably, the element fire, which in our ordinary observation is destructive rather than life-giving, is less suitable for the role of creative, causative matter than *pneuma*. This development leaves many details obscure, though. What is the relationship between the pure fire of conflagration (which Chrysippus and most of his followers continued to believe in) and the creative *pneuma* that ensues? And if *pneuma* is a special compound of fire and air, how can it be fundamental to other things? How are the elements related to *pneuma*? Surely their emergence is not guided by *pneuma*, which is a compound of them.

The sources we possess just don't suffice to settle all of these questions, but nonetheless the basic picture of Stoic cosmology outlined here is one that the school stayed with throughout its long history. The most important features of Stoic physics all fit within this basic outline. These core physical doctrines include the elaborate and orderly classification of the various kinds of entities in the world, a variety which needed to be tamed in order to maintain the strong unity of the cosmos which lay at the heart of their theory. There are, as indicated earlier, four levels of such entities, distinguished by the kinds of capacities which they exhibit (see Figure 3). The simplest beings are inert (minerals, for example) and their essential capacity is merely the possession of basic attributes and the ability to hold themselves together as unified objects. This holding together and possession of basic attributes is described as their *hexis* (a term derived from the Greek verb 'to have' which also has the sense of 'being in a certain condition' and even 'cohesion'). More elaborate are things that can grow, nourish themselves, and reproduce. Plants are the best examples, and they are held together and kept alive (for they are alive in a way that minerals are not) by their *phusis* (or 'nature'; the Greek term is derived from the word 'to grow' and translated into Latin as *natura*). Plants are not self-moving and don't

perfect *logos*	GOD(S) (AND THE SAGE)
logos	HUMANS
psuchē	NON-RATIONAL ANIMALS
phusis	PLANTS
hexis	NON-LIVING STUFF (MINERALS, ETC.)

3. The 'scala naturae'.

perceive, although they do react to their environments in limited ways. Perceptual self-movers are animals, and the principle that makes them what they are is not just a nature (though that term always has a general sense as well as its specific meaning) but a 'soul' or *psuchē*. Things with soul, animals, have more powers than just nourishment and reproduction; they can also perceive, desire, and move themselves. Animals, such as humans, whose soul is even more sophisticated in virtue of having rationality can be said to be what they are because of reason (*logos*), by which is meant the rational soul. Rational animals (mature humans are the most familiar instances) do everything that lower entities do but do so rationally. That means that we have the capacity to respond critically to our perceptions and to process and manipulate them as well. Consequently we humans have not just the ability to fit into the pattern of the world, as all entities do, but also the ability to understand that we do so and to make efforts to enhance that fit. More on that later, in Chapter 5 on ethics and in Chapter 6 when we discuss the 'use of impressions'.

The unity of the world is maintained by the physical makeup of these four kinds of being. For at each level things are held together (sustained in being) and endowed with their qualities and capacities in virtue of the same thing, the relevant form of *pneuma*. The differences between rocks, plants, animals, and humans are all attributable to differences in the form of the *pneuma* that shapes the raw material in them. The feature of *pneuma* that makes all these differences is its tension (*tonos*). In physical terms, the cohesive elasticity of the *pneuma* which all entities share is what defines them. And this *pneuma* is also the basic active principle which permeates the whole cosmos and is labelled Nature in a more global sense than that which characterizes individual entities. This Nature is also what makes the world a living thing, its 'world soul' as a Platonist might say; and it is also a divine, therefore rational, soul. The Stoics can, as a result, regard the entire cosmos as a rational animal, formed on the same principles as each of the entities which forms a part of it.

Human beings have a *pneuma* whose tension (*tonos*) is closest to that of the cosmos as a whole, and in principle the same in kind as it, which makes us privileged parts of the world.

The entire physical theory rests on a pervasive contrast between what is active (fire, air, or *pneuma*) and what is passive (the rest of the elements). This polarity is found in rocks, plants, animals (where it is the contrast between body and soul), humans, and the world. At the most abstract level, then, the world can be described as an interaction between an active principle and a passive principle. These principles (*archai*) are never found in isolation from each other, except perhaps at the moment of conflagration, as there is only active fire in existence at that point; but they provide a useful framework for analysis of everything in nature. In that sense these principles are helpfully thought of as metaphysical, not because they transcend nature altogether but because they pervade it in a way that goes beyond the particular nature of any individual object. Despite that, there is nothing incorporeal about the principles. (Our sources appear to differ on this, but in my view the right way to resolve the disagreement is by remembering that for Stoics anything that either causes or is caused must be corporeal.) The whole idea of acting and being acted upon demands that things involved be physical, as we saw in Chapter 3. The Giants of Plato's *Sophist* haven't gone away.

Another prominent 'metaphysical' feature of Stoic physics is their doctrine of 'categories'—a misleading term borrowed from the Aristotelian tradition but one that is by now too well-entrenched to abandon. The Stoics themselves seem to have called these 'categories' *kinds of beings (genē tōn ontōn)*; the fact that they involve *being* shows that they too must be bodily. It helps to think of these kinds as features or aspects of ordinary entities. The first of these is the substrate or matter of things (*hupokeimenon, hulē*). In itself matter has no determinate features; it is just the raw material out of which everything is made—it's not as though you ever find such utterly unqualified matter (*apoios hulē*) in existence on its own, but it is a feature of things that can be isolated for analysis. The second 'category' is the particular quality that makes each bit of matter into the thing that it is (a peculiar quality or *idiōs poion*). In these two we see the passive and active aspect of any determinate thing, a bit of raw material and the active, shaping element that holds it together and makes it what it is. (The Stoics also recognized 'common qualities', which represent the shared features of things which fall into the same kind or type—Socrates has a peculiar quality which makes him Socrates, but the features which he shares with other humans are 'common qualities', a subset of the features that are peculiar to him as an individual.) The third 'category' presupposes the presence of such a determinate thing and picks out the state that it is in: its 'disposition' (*pōs echon*). A human being (say, Socrates) is the peculiar quality of a bit of matter, in this case his soul in contrast to his body which is his matter. But the various dispositions and conditions that Socrates has, whether long-lasting like 'wisdom' or short-lived like 'sunburnt', are his dispositions, specifications of what sort of condition he's in. The final 'category' is not so much a feature of such an object on its own but of its relationship to other things in the organized world, its 'relative dispositions' (*pros ti pōs echonta*). If Socrates is *beside* Cebes or *shorter than* Simmias or the *husband of* Xanthippe, these are all relative dispositions.

It may seem odd to describe these as kinds of being, when despite the presence of all four there is really only one entity (in this case, Socrates). He has a material, passive aspect and a soul that makes him what he is, though of course he also has properties that accompany his basic being without generating an extra entity in the world—even less so would his relative properties do so. So it is best to think of these 'categories' as picking out aspects of the unified physical world for analysis and description; in that sense they may seem metaphysical or even 'logical' (since they indicate ways we can and do talk about things in the world). What these 'categories' or kinds of being do not do, definitely, is weaken the unity and integration of the world and its contents. If, as seems overwhelmingly likely, the peculiar quality is the bit of tensed *pneuma* that makes a thing what it is, then the ubiquity and coordination of all the *pneuma* in the world further supports the cohesion and unity of the cosmos which the Stoics aimed to recognize in their physical system.

Another unifying aspect of the Stoic cosmos is their theory of causation. As Giants, they recognized that only matter can act or be acted upon, and so all causes are relationships between bodies. And since, as most ancient philosophers agreed, there can be no uncaused events or entities, if the all-pervasive, rational power of divine *pneuma* is what causes things to be what they are and do what they do, there must be, if only at a very high level of abstraction, a single coordinated network of causes and effects that permeate the world and structure all of its events, just as there is a single, coordinated active principle in the world, which is called Nature, god, or Zeus. That means as well that all the events and objects in the world are connected with each other in a holistic way (a form of connection that they called *sumpatheia*). Some causal connections they recognized as part of this cosmic sympathy we still recognize as valid (such as the effect of the moon on tides noted by Posidonius), others are now regarded as unscientific (for example, the effect of the heavenly bodies on human lives recognized by astrology): such is the progress of science! The coordinated causal network recognized by Stoic physics is also a rational construction, and not just in the sense that it is subject to analysis and comprehension. The Stoics also claimed that this rational causal network (or fate, as they termed it) was part of a purposive plan. Not only, then, are the Stoics determinists (perhaps the earliest determinists of the western tradition) but they are also *providential* determinists.

Determinism in its Stoic form is a demanding and controversial doctrine. It's one thing to hold that there are no uncaused events in the world, but it is something else again to make this claim in the Stoic way, holding that everything that happens in the world is also part of a *coordinated* network of causes, effects, events, and objects, and that this network is the expression of a master plan aimed at the best possible outcome. There are many philosophical objections to this form of determinism, but two in particular stand out. If everything is caused, what about human actions? Are my actions, decisions, and even my thoughts (which, for materialists like the Stoics, are also material events) determined in advanced by the 'will of Zeus'? Does that mean that in some sense I am not free to make real choices, that I am a sort of puppet? That's one objection. The other concerns all the bad things that go on in the world. If the all-pervasive network of causes and effects is the expression of a providential plan aimed at producing the good, how does it come about that there is so much badness in the world? For to any reasonable observer it certainly looks as though there is a whole lot of badness out there: not only plagues, poverty, war, etc., but also bad people, vicious character traits, and the frustration of good intentions. If there is a divine plan causing everything in the world, why isn't everything perfect, or at least a great deal better than it seems to be? (This is an issue of particular interest to Marcus Aurelius, as we saw at the beginning of this book, but all Stoics had to deal with it in one way or another.)

To the first objection, Stoics had a powerful philosophical response. Starting at least with Chrysippus they developed a version of a position now labelled 'compatibilism', which maintains that full causal determination is compatible with meaningful choices made by human beings. Our actions, the Stoics proposed, are the product of two factors, stimuli from our environmental circumstances (usually referred to as 'impressions') and reactions determined by the state of our minds, our characters; a positive reaction, assent, leads to action, but assent can be withheld. One test of causal determination is the hypothetical question: if the same situation occurs again will there be the same outcome? And the Stoics held that the answer is yes. Given my character and the options set before me, the choice I make is determined and, in principle, predictable. But, they contend, my agency is not threatened because the key factor here is *my* character; what makes the difference between one outcome and another is the decision *I* come to, based on *my* personality, dispositions, awareness of relevant facts, etc. Anyone else facing the same situation will react differently, in accordance with who they are and what they know. In that way, even though my actions are causally determined, they are very much my own; personal agency is preserved. The Stoics illustrated their theory with the analogy of two objects, a cone and cylinder, being pushed down a hill. (See Box 3 and Figure 4.) The external stimulus (the push) is

Box 3 Cicero, *On Fate*

For although assent cannot occur unless it is set in motion by an impression, nevertheless since the impression has in it a proximate cause rather than a principal cause it can be accounted for in the way that we have been talking about for some time now, in accordance with Chrysippus' wish. It's not that assent could occur if it weren't stirred up by some force from the outside (for it is necessary that assent be set in motion by an impression), but he falls back on that cylinder and cone of his, things which cannot be initially set in motion unless they are struck. But when that does happen he thinks that from then on it is by their own natures that the cylinder rolls and the cone spins. He says,

> so just as the person who pushed the cylinder gave it the start of its motion but did not give it its tendency to roll, so too an impression which is encountered will certainly make an impact and as it were stamp its form on the mind, but assent will be in our power; and the assent, just as we said in the case of the cylinder, when struck from the outside will from then on move in accordance with its own force and nature. But if anything were to occur without any antecedent cause then it would be false that everything happens by fate. (42–3)

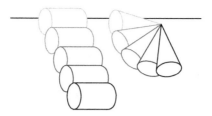

4. '…it is by their own natures that the cylinder rolls and the cone spins'. (Cicero, *On Fate* 42)

not in the objects' control, but the way they react (rolling straight or wobbling around) is determined by their own unique shapes, that is, by what they are at the time of the stimulus.

But one might well wonder whether that preserves human freedom; agency might be safe, but it might seem to be a rather unfree sort of agency, barely worthy of the name. In reply, a Stoic will press his critic on what *they* mean by freedom. Are they looking for some sort of radical indeterminacy, so that we are in a position to decide to do absolutely anything on any occasion, regardless of our personality, character, state of knowledge, or prior inclinations and commitments? Is that really what we value, the chance to act randomly and without motivation or connection to our own past and present character (as though some random mental event, such as the 'swerve' posited by the Epicureans, led to our choice)? If so, then Stoics, who think that it is markedly better to do things for reasons and not at random, will cheerfully reject that sort of freedom. But what would happen, we might still ask them, if we faced a choice about how to act and were paralysed by knowing that the outcome was already fixed? Here the Stoics reply with a distinction. We do know that at some level the outcome is fixed—they are determinists, after all. But we humans (unlike Zeus) don't and can't know what the outcome is in any particular case. We don't have complete and in-depth knowledge of our own characters and inclinations; we have only a partial grasp of the circumstances relevant to the choice we face. So as rational agents we still have to think through as best we can what the right thing to do is. That some ideal and perfectly informed observer (such as a mind-reading Zeus?) might be able to predict what I am going to decide doesn't change the fact that the decision is one that *I* make—and just as important, that it is a decision for which I can reasonably be held accountable. My actions are expressions of who I am and how I reason, so I get credit for good choices and blame for bad ones.

But hold on. Critics of compatibilism come back with one more objection. Our characters are not wholly of our own making, are they? We owe what we are to our physical inheritance, our early education, our social situation, the choices we made before we had enough rationality to be taken seriously as moral agents, and many other factors beyond our control. So if this character of mine makes a good or bad decision, the credit or blame surely doesn't go to *me* but to that network of influences and causes that make my character what it is. The network of fated events doesn't just present me with the external circumstances in which I have to act, but it also presents me with my character. How can it be fair to assign either praise or blame to *me* rather than to my physical makeup, my parents, my school, my neighbourhood, and so on? The Stoics have, I think, a straightforward and tough-minded answer to this. Who or what am I, over and above my character and personality? There is no distinct inner 'me' that could confront the influence of my character. I just am my character and so what my character does is mine. No one is the complete cause of his or her own character; we are all products of our past and our environment. So there really isn't a problem, here, replies the Stoic. Each of us just is what he or she is, no matter how we got here. If our character is weak or wicked, then we might well think that the world is unfair. But as we will see, the Stoic theory of human nature also has a deeply optimistic streak in it: no matter what our character is like now, being a rational human being means that we also have in our character the capacity for improvement. If we do find a way to draw on that capacity and make the right sorts of decisions over and over again then we will become better people, but even in that scenario there will be no uncaused actions. In conjunction with external influences and causes we can engage in self-improvement and in that way cooperate with the larger plan for generating goodness in the cosmos. Of course, it is in fact predetermined who will make this effort and whether it will succeed, but we don't and can't know who in particular will in fact try and whether he or she will succeed. If we knew this sort of thing then we might well be paralysed, not to mention depressed. But given the limits on human knowledge about these particulars we just carry on acting in a characteristically human fashion, that is, rationally but with limited information.

That is the genuine Stoic position on this problem, but it's very likely that at least one Stoic thinker, the emperor Marcus Aurelius, wasn't fully satisfied by it—and who can blame him? At times Marcus writes, in his philosophical diary, as though there is in fact an inner self distinct from the character determined by the causal sequence of fate. If that is his view (see Box 4 for texts suggesting this) then we have to admit that he broke free from the teachings of his Stoic predecessors in a more radical way than is sometimes appreciated. Maybe his anticipation of such a modern-seeming conception of the self that is somehow free from the specified causal chain helps to explain his perennial appeal to readers. Either way, the Stoic account is seemingly left with the need to give a satisfactory explanation of accountability—a concept that may appear to imply a 'self' distinct from the network of physical and social causes.

But there is still the other objection to the Stoic theory. If the determined world is part of a grand plan aimed at producing the good, why is there so much bad in the world? The Stoic theory provoked an early version of the perennial 'problem of evil' that would trouble and perplex religious thinkers for centuries to come. But they didn't pioneer this problem.

Box 4 Marcus Aurelius, *To Himself*

Whatever it is that I am, this is just flesh, a bit of breath [*pneumation*], and my 'leading part' [*hēgemonikon*].... As though already dying, hold the flesh in contempt. It is nothing but gore and bones and an interwoven mesh of sinews, veins and arteries. Think, too, about what kind of a thing your breath is: mere wind, and not even the same over time; at every moment it is spewed out and then gulped back down again. So the third thing is our leading part. (2.2)

Body, soul, mind: sense-impressions belong to the body, impulses to the soul, and judgements to the mind.... (3.16)

You are composed of three things: body, breath, and mind. The first two belong to you in so far as you need to take care of them, but only the third is yours in the proper sense. So if you detach from yourself, that is, from your own mind, whatever other people do or say or whatever you yourself have done or said, and all the anticipations of the future that disturb you and all the extraneous involuntary aspects of the body that envelops you or of your inborn breath, and all the twistings of the external vortex that whirls around you—so that your intellectual faculty can live in a pure condition, exempt from co-fated events, unfettered and independent, doing just deeds, welcoming what actually happens, and speaking the truth. If, as I say, you detach from this 'leading part' everything that gets glued on to it by passionate experiences and by everything that is in future or past time and if you make yourself, in the words of Empedocles, 'a well-rounded sphere, rejoicing in its circular solitude' and if you practise living only in what you really live, that is, the present—then you will be able to live out the time that is left until you die in a manner that is free of upset and good-natured, at peace with your own divine spirit [*daimōn*]. (12.3)

The credit for that goes to Plato, or rather to his character 'Timaeus' in the dialogue named for him. In his 'likely story' (which is how Timaeus describes it) about the origin and nature of the cosmos, Timaeus has a craftsman god create things, motivated always to produce as much good as possible. The defects and failings of the world that might, however, lead us to wonder about the origin of evil cannot be pinned on god. After all, the craftsman god is not all-powerful. Like any other craftworker, god has to make the best product that he can with the materials available to him. Recalcitrant matter means that, literally with the best will in the world, there are bound to be bad outcomes. That doesn't mean that the world isn't as good as it can be—the best of all possible worlds. It's just that the best possible world is perhaps not good enough for critics inflamed by the desire for perfection. For a Platonist, though, perfection is not to be expected in the physical world.

The problem of evil is tougher for the Stoics. Though their cosmology and physical theory owed a great deal to Plato and especially to the *Timaeus*, the Stoics were still Giants, that is, materialists. God himself, though a rational craftsman, is material. In fact, in Stoic cosmology god's fiery substance is the sole starting point and raw material for the world. All of the earth, air, fire, and water of this cosmos have their origin in god's pure fire (which transforms itself into other elements in the way outlined earlier in this chapter); and so too does the *pneuma* which makes up human souls. So if there are defects in the world, where else can they originate except in god? And isn't god perfect and motivated to produce only good? One can see quickly how Stoicism already comes perilously close to the Christian version of the problem of evil, a problem dominated by the religious belief that god is omnipotent—and so, presumably, responsible for everything that happens in the world, even the bad parts.

What do the Stoics have to say for themselves? Alas, their answers do not represent their finest work. Sometimes they seem to be helping themselves to Plato's solution, treating the Stoic god as one that is somehow constrained by the raw material he has to work with—as though he weren't also the source of that raw material. And at other times they even suggest that god actually wants a bit of badness in the world, to provide balance and contrast, and so to generate a kind of harmony of opposites which is itself good in some higher respect (see Box 5 for a passage from Cleanthes suggesting this). Some Stoics (like Seneca, see Box 6) even suggest that the presence of bad things in the world is helpful, providing humans with the chance to develop virtues and in that way to generate more goodness. A somewhat shifty way of responding to the problem of evil becomes apparent when Stoics define goodness and badness (which is the same term that we sometimes translate as 'evil') in their own distinctively narrow way. If the only real good is virtue and the only genuinely bad thing is vice, then maybe god is blameless, since we are at least partly responsible for our own character development.

Box 5 Cleanthes, *Hymn to Zeus*

Nor does anything happen on earth without you, god,
Nor in the ethereal and divine heaven nor on the sea,
Except for what bad men do in their own folly.
But you know how to make the crooked straight
And to bring order to what is disorderly; the unlovable is loved
    by you.
For this is how you have harmonized all into one, the good with
    the bad,
So that there is one eternal rational principle for all things;
Because they flee from and neglect this principle, all the mortals
    who are bad
Are wretched and though they yearn to possess good things
They do not see the universal law of god, nor do they hear it,
Though if they obeyed it they would live a good life with
    discernment. (11–27)

Box 6 Seneca, *On Providence*

Lucilius, you have asked me why it is that if the world is run by providence many bad things happen to good men... (1.1)

Nothing bad *can* happen to a good man. Opposites do not mix. Just as all those rivers, all that rain falling from above, all those polluted springs cannot change the taste of the sea, cannot even dilute it, so too the onset of adverse circumstances does not alter the mind of a brave man. He remains in his own condition and converts everything that comes along into his own state. For he is stronger than all external circumstances. I don't say that he doesn't feel the adversities, but he conquers them and though he is otherwise tranquil and calm he rises up when facing an attack... (2.1–2)

God has an exceptional love for good men and wants them to be as good and as outstanding as possible; are you then surprised that he sends them misfortune to exercise themselves on? I'm certainly not surprised if the gods sometimes want to see great men wrestling with disaster... (2.7)

As my discussion proceeds I will show that apparently bad things are not bad. For now I will just say that the things that you call harsh, adverse, or deplorable are, in the first place, to the advantage of those whom they befall and, secondly, that they are to the advantage of people in general (for whom the gods have a greater concern than they do for individuals) and then that these things befall men who embrace them, and if they don't then they deserve the bad outcome. I will add to this the fact that these things occur by fate and befall good men in accordance with the same law by which they are good. Then

(*Continued*)

Box 6 Continued

I will persuade you never to feel sorry for a good man; he can be called miserable, but he cannot be so.... (3.1)

Among all the inspiring utterances of our Demetrius here is one that I heard recently—it is still ringing and echoing in my ears: Nothing seems more unfortunate than a man who has faced no adversity. For he has never had the chance to test himself... (3.3)

Fortunate circumstances come to the mob and low-grade minds. But it is distinctive of a great man to subdue the disasters and panics of mortal men. Indeed, to be lucky all the time and to go through life without mental distress is to remain ignorant of half of the natural world. (4.1)

But why has god been so unfair in the distribution of fate that he inflicted poverty, wounds, and premature deaths on good men? The craftsman cannot change his raw material. Nature hasn't permitted this. Some things cannot be separated one from another, they stick together, they're inseparable. Slothful characters, people always nodding off or maintaining a wakefulness not better than sleep, are composed of lazy elements. In order to make a man who can seriously be called a man you need a sterner fate. He won't have a smooth path; he must go uphill and down; he must be storm-tossed and steer his ship amidst the turmoil. He must hold his course in the face of fortune. He will face much that is harsh and bitter, but he will tame it and smooth it out. It is fire that proves the gold; it is misery that proves brave men. (5.9)

Ultimately, though, that sort of answer will not satisfy critics, nor should it. With god as the only rational principle in the universe, the very setup of the problem can be laid at his door. It does not help to say that (for example) disease and disaster aren't strictly speaking bad so it's no problem if the world is full of such regrettable circumstances and to add that therefore the real problem is our human response to such circumstances. A good god with the kind of monopoly on cosmic causation that Zeus has could surely have done a better job than this! Without the excuse provided by the limited power of the Platonic Demiurge and the *ultimate* recalcitrance of matter, the Stoic god seems to be vulnerable to an insuperable objection.

We have been discussing the world of cause and effect, which is the world of matter, and some of the philosophical challenges that the Stoics face as a result of their commitment to materialism and determinism. But the Stoic world is not limited to material entities. As we have seen, in addition to causally significant bodies, the world also contains entities of a non-bodily sort, which are therefore unable to exert causal influence or to be affected by causes. What these incorporeals do, however, is to enable Stoics to give a fully articulated account, a *logos*, of how the world operates. 'Sayables' (i.e. the intelligible content accompanying various physical states such as sense impressions) cause nothing, and neither do place, void, and time. But without place and time the Stoics thought that they wouldn't be able to account for the movements and changes that bodies undergo. We have to be able to say that body B is now where body A used to be, or vice versa. The location occupied first by A and then by B has to have some standing or such changes couldn't be described. And so too for the times at which things occur. The theoretical usefulness of place and time extends beyond such simple examples, but even this much shows that the Stoics were right to think that the incorporeals deserve a place in their physical system, even though neither they nor we would think that void, place, and time are actual causes.

What about void, which is nothing more than unoccupied place? Here we need to recall one other difference between Stoic cosmology and Aristotle's. Outside the cosmos, Aristotle thought, there is nothing. Even the unmoved mover is not in a place; it is, of course, non-material. But the Stoic cosmos is surrounded by emptiness, void. Why, one might wonder, would the otherwise parsimonious Stoics add such a thing to their metaphysical theory? For the answer, we have to think back to their theory of universal conflagration. If the whole cosmos is going to go up in flames at some future time, then like anything else that is heated and bursts into flame it will take up more space—it will expand. So there must be some unoccupied space outside the cosmos to accommodate this expansion—and that seems to be the only reason for postulating void. Certainly no Stoic accepted that there could be void within the cosmos; as Aristotle also held, when bodies move around they do so by switching places all at the same time, not by coming to occupy previously void locations as the atomists thought. Void, while recognized by Stoics, is the smallest of footnotes in their physical theory.

Sayables are something else again, and we will have to come back to them when we consider some features of Stoic logic. But for now the most important point has to do with their theory of human psychology and communication. Perceiving, thinking, and communicating are all parts of causal relationships that involve the human mind (the rational soul). As a material object, the soul can act and be acted upon. When we perceive or think or speak we are aware of content, as modern philosophers of mind would say. For the Stoics, intelligible content is something that only rational animals have access to—the term for 'sayable', *lekton*, is etymologically linked to the word *logos*, reason or discourse. Perceptions and mental events that cause behaviour in non-animals do so at a merely causal level, without any access to intelligible content; but mature humans have an awareness of the mental content that accompanies all such physical processes in the mind or that affect the mind. Access to content is precisely what makes us rational and, on the Stoic view, enables us to do things with a self-starting flexibility that other creatures do not have. (See Box 7.) It's not that the contents we have access to cause anything, but like

Box 7 Epictetus, *Discourse*

You will not find any of our other capacities that contemplates itself and so none that either approves or disapproves of itself upon scrutiny. To what extent does grammar possess the power of contemplation? To the extent that it can make distinctions among writings. Music? To the extent that it can make distinctions among tunes. Does any of them contemplate itself? Not at all. But when you need to know what to write, if you are writing to your friend, then grammar will tell you. But as to whether or not you should be writing to your friend, that grammar will not tell you. It is the same with tunes and music. It won't tell you whether you should sing and play the kithara now or not. So what will tell you? A capacity which contemplates both itself and everything else. And what capacity is this? The reasoning capacity. For this is the only capacity which we have received that can come to an understanding of itself (what it is and what it can do and what value it comes to us with) and also of all our other capacities. For what else is it which tells us that gold is beautiful? The gold doesn't tell us itself. Obviously it is the capacity which makes use of impressions. What else is it that draws distinctions about music, grammar, and all the other capacities, approving how they are used and indicating the right time to use them? Nothing else but the reasoning capacity.

So, as was right, the gods have made only the most powerful and dominant of all capacities up to us, the

(Continued)

Box 7 Continued

correct use of impressions. They did not make the others
up to us. Is that because they didn't want to? My own
view is that if they were able to they would have entrusted
them to us. But they just couldn't. Given that we are
earthbound and tied to a body such as ours is and to
companions of the kind we have, how could it be possible
for us not to be hindered by externals in these
respects? (1.1.1–9)

place, time, and void they are non-physical realities in the world
without which, they thought, their theory could not account for the
causes and effects which do occur. Our minds, the Stoics thought,
operate and interact with the world by corporeal causation, but
without sayables we wouldn't be able to give a proper account of
what is so obviously distinctive of human thought and action.

Chapter 5
Ethics

Whether or not it was the culminating point of their philosophy for ancient Stoics, ethics is the part of their legacy which is most prominent and influential today. In broad outline, their theory of the good life for human beings, which is what ethics by and large amounted to for most ancient philosophers, falls into the family of theories associated with Socrates and his followers. This tradition includes Plato and most Platonists, Xenophon, the Cynics, Aristotle and later Aristotelians, all of whom share the view that virtue, the excellence of a human being, is the highest value and (as we would say) is its own reward. It stands in contrast with a tradition, going back to some of the sophists in the 5th century BCE, that values the virtues essentially for their ability to help us to obtain other good things, such as pleasure, wealth, social recognition, and personal safety. That instrumentalist theory of virtue was best represented in the Hellenistic and later periods by Epicureans, who are the most consistent foil for Stoics in this area. The distinctive position of the Stoics becomes clearer if we think of the challenge put to Socrates at the beginning of book 2 of Plato's *Republic*. Is justice valued and worth pursuing (a) because of the extrinsic benefits it produces; (b) because of the intrinsic benefits it produces; or (c) because of both? An Epicurean chooses option (a); Plato, Aristotle, and most other ancient theorists choose (c); Stoics choose (b). Not only is virtue its own reward, but any additional benefits it might produce are not similarly valuable and cannot be a reason for choosing virtue. In fact, most Stoics would say that it would somehow degrade or taint virtue to choose it even in part for that sort of reason. Stoics aren't alone in taking this extreme and even counter-intuitive position—the loosely defined group known as Cynics would join them and push the paradoxes even further on occasion; but Stoicism is the school that provides the best worked out and most credible version of the position.

As we saw earlier, it is difficult to separate any branch of Stoic philosophy from the others. Ethics focuses on the best way of life for rational animals, and for that reason it is entangled with logic, which in its broadest sense is the study of *logos*, the characteristic which makes humans rational. It certainly cannot be separated from physics, the study of the unified and rationally ordered natural world and its governance. The rational power pervading the world is providential, in the sense that it aims to produce goodness wherever it can. As rational animals, human beings are a part of this system, and the Stoics in various contexts described humans as *parts of the whole*, for whom it is either inappropriate or impossible to defy the system they fit into, or as the *children of Zeus*, who are bound by filial piety to follow the lead of Zeus, father of gods and men (the Stoics loved adopting and repurposing Homeric notions). However this relationship is described, it comes along with the further and essential claim that Nature endows human beings with certain basic properties and capacities. These elements in human nature include innate inclinations which we are programmed to follow and which we *must* follow and perfect if we are ever to be fully successful versions of ourselves (that is, to achieve our goal, happiness). These inclinations include a powerful bias in favour of virtue and the good (the only truly advantageous thing), a natural affiliation with other human beings (our basic social nature), and our attachment to reason and truth. (See Box 8 for a passage of

Box 8 Epictetus, *Discourse*

What is the cause of assenting to something? The
impression that it is the case. For it is not possible to
assent to something that does not give the impression
of being the case. Why is this? Because this is the
nature of the mind, to agree with what is true and to
be discontented with what is false, and to suspend
judgement about what is unclear. 'Why should we believe
this?' If you can, have the feeling that it is now night. 'Not
possible.' Get rid of the feeling that it is day. 'Not possible.'
Either feel or don't feel that the number of stars is even.
'Not possible.' So, when someone assents to something
false, be assured that he did not want to assent to
something false. For every soul is unwillingly deprived of
truth, as Plato says. Rather, it thought that the falsehood
was true.

Well then, in the sphere of actions what do we have that is
similar to truth and falsehood in this area? The appropriate
and inappropriate, the advantageous and disadvantageous,
what suits me and doesn't suit me, and things like that. 'So
cannot someone think that something is advantageous for
himself and yet not choose it?' No, he can't. 'What about
the woman [i.e., Medea] who says, "I know the kind of evils
I am going to commit, but my anger is stronger than my
deliberations"?' It's because she thinks that this, indulging
her anger and taking revenge on her husband, is more
advantageous than saving her children. 'Yes, but she is
wrong about that.' Show her clearly that she is wrong and
then she won't do it. But until you do show her, what can
she follow except what seems to be the case? Nothing.
(1.28.1–8)

Epictetus emphasizing that humans pursue such goals by nature and so necessarily.)

The claim that Nature has made human beings on these principles and with these built-in inclinations can be seen in two ways. If we think of Nature, or Zeus, in very concrete and personal terms as a Craftsman god, then we are literally his creatures and it can begin to sound rather like the relationship between human beings and the creator god of the Judeo-Christian tradition, someone whose gifts we strive to use well. But if we think of Nature more impersonally as the rational and orderly plan and pattern that governs a world of physical cause and effect, then instead of seeing these attributes as the gifts of a god to his creatures we will think of our social, rational, and integrated nature as a set of facts governing our lives and the conditions for human fulfilment. Some Stoics (Cleanthes, Epictetus, and Marcus Aurelius) inclined to the more personal and 'theological' way of looking at things, whereas others (Chrysippus and Posidonius) seem to have taken a more detached, 'scientific' stance. But these are merely differences of emphasis and expression, since it is common to the entire school to regard the natural world as orderly and rule-governed and also as infused with divine purpose.

Even when viewed from the less personalized perspective, human nature is defined teleologically, in terms of its built-in purpose or function, and this function is fundamental to Stoic ethics. And just as fundamental is the conviction that human nature is a fully integrated component of Nature as a whole, and not just a part of Nature but a privileged part. Human rationality is held to be the same in kind as the rationality that administers the world. That sameness in kind is the basis of our ability to *understand* the world as it unfolds in accordance with the rational plan and also the reason why it is in our nature to *align* ourselves with it. The idea that human nature is fulfilled by 'following' Nature or living in harmony with it (the most common Stoic expression of the goal of human life) follows from this way of looking at the place of human beings in the cosmos.

Plato and Aristotle would agree with much of this. Aristotle famously aimed to connect the goal of human life, its *telos*, with the natural function of the human species and he certainly believed that our nature as rational and social (indeed, political) animals is fundamental to any account of human virtue and happiness. It is more difficult to extract a single view about these issues from Plato's dialogues, but when later Platonists seized on the notion that the goal for human life is to become like god (*homoiōsis theōi*) they were not far off the mark. In fact, the more theological side of Stoicism owes a good deal to Platonic inspiration; Stoics and Platonists (and even Aristotle, though less flamboyantly) thought of human rationality as a godlike trait and of human improvement as a matter of becoming more and more like god. (Stoics and Aristotelians tended to avoid, however, the low regard verging on contempt for the corporeal and physical side of life which characterized some Platonists.)

As parts of the cosmic system, human beings strive for the good, and the good for human beings is our characteristic excellence. The Greek term we conventionally translate as 'virtue' is *aretē*, the original sense of which is simply 'excellence'; it did not involve any restricted or special sense of 'morality', as the term 'virtue' tends to do for us. Ancient Greek ethics thus has a subtly different focus from what we are most accustomed to today. Whereas we might well ask 'why should I be virtuous?' that question wouldn't make sense in the teleological framework of ancient ethics. Their version of the question, 'Why should I be excellent?' would seem pointless. (Plato did explore why one would want to be *just*, but once it is clear that justice is in fact an excellence, rather than a foolish naivety, as some sophists thought, the debate is quickly over.) Fulfilling one's true nature as best one can is simply what it means to be active as a member of one's natural kind. Instead, the ancients would be more likely to ask what virtue is and what it involves. So the corresponding question would be, 'what is virtue?' or 'what are the virtues?' The claim that justice, for example, is a virtue is tantamount to the claim that excellence as a human being requires that one be just, and that figuring out what justice demands is a top priority for us. But once that is established there would be no point in asking whether you *want* to be just—of course you do; it's part of what you are. It follows from this approach to the virtues that understanding them and what they demand requires that we understand human nature, for that is what tells us how to be excellent at being human.

The Stoics followed Plato (in the *Republic*, at least) in accepting that there are four basic virtues: justice, courage, wisdom, and moderation or self-control (*sōphrosunē*). The ways in which these basic virtues are rooted in human nature are fairly clear, and it is particularly useful to look at the way Panaetius connected them up with our nature (as reported in Cicero's *On Duties* book 1; see Box 9).

Box 9 Cicero, *On Duties*

In the first place, nature has granted to every animal species that they should protect themselves, their life and their body, avoid those things which seem likely to cause them harm, and seek out and acquire the necessities of life (such as food, shelter and so forth). All animals also share the desire for intercourse for the sake of procreation and a measure of care for their offspring. The biggest difference between humans and beasts is that the latter, in so far as they are only moved by the senses, respond only to what is at hand in the present, being barely aware of past or future. Humans, though, have reason, which enables them to see consequences, and so they can discern the causes of things, and they are aware of their preconditions and antecedents. Humans make comparisons among similar things, linking and connecting future situations to the present, easily grasping the whole span of life and making ready what is necessary for living that life. That same nature links one human being to another through the power of reason, so that they share both speech and life. Above all, nature creates in humans an exceptional love for their offspring and drives them to want there to be meetings and gatherings among people and to join in them, and for this reason people are eager to provide for the support and sustenance not only of themselves but also for their wives and children and others whom they hold dear and are obliged to protect. This concern stimulates their spirit and makes them more effective at getting things done. [This is the foundation for the virtue of justice.]

It is, first and foremost, characteristic of human beings to seek and probe for the truth. [This is the virtue of wisdom.] And so when we are free from mandatory duties and concerns we are keen to see, hear, and learn things and we think that knowledge of arcane or wondrous things is indispensable for the happy life. From this you can conclude that whatever is true, simple, and pure is most suited to human nature. Connected to this drive for seeing the truth is a kind of lust for leadership: no mind that has been formed properly by nature is willing to defer to anyone except a teacher or instructor or a just and lawful commander acting in the interests of utility. This is the source of greatness of soul and the ability to look down on merely human affairs. [Some Stoics, and Plato, call this virtue courage rather than greatness of soul.] And it is no small part of the impact of nature and reason that humans are the only animal that perceives what

(Continued)

Box 9 Continued

orderliness is, what is fitting, and where balance lies in actions and discourse. So no other animal sees in the things perceived by vision their beauty, their charm, and the harmony among their parts. Nature and reason transfer a version of this from the eyes to the mind, in the conviction that beauty, consistency, and orderliness are even more worth preserving in the domain of deliberation and action, and they are to do nothing that is unseemly or effeminate and that in all our thoughts and deeds there should be nothing motivated by lust. [This is the virtue of self-control, or temperance.]

These are the components that make up the honourable which we are seeking. And even if it is not publicly recognized it is still honourable and, as we rightly claim, even if no one praises it nevertheless it is praiseworthy by nature. There you see, my son Marcus, the very form and as it were the face of the honourable. If it could be seen with the eyes it would, as Plato says, arouse an astonishing love of wisdom. But everything that is honourable arises from one of these four parts. For either it deals with the grasp of truth and intelligence, or with the protection of human society, the distribution to each person of his due and the sanctity of contracts, or with the greatness and strength of a lofty and undefeated soul, or with the orderliness and limit of everything that is done and said (which involves modesty and self-control). Although these four are linked together and interwoven with each other, nevertheless distinct kinds of responsibility emerge from each of them; for example, in the first part described, where we located wisdom and prudence, is found the search for and discovery of the truth and this is the distinctive function of this virtue. (1.11–15)

More generally, though, our nature as rational and social animals is the key factor in determining what the virtues are and what they demand. Since we are rational, all of our actions should manifest perfected reason if they are to be the best they can be; and perfected reason is the excellence the Stoics labelled 'wisdom'. And since we are naturally social, justice should permeate all that we do (though of course we also have to use our wisdom to get a proper understanding of the demands that justice makes of us). Courage and self-control are required in order to be virtuous; any difficult action (including standing up for our fellow humans or for our country in accordance with justice) demands that we persist in the face of dangers and obstacles; and this is courage. Any other-regarding social action requires that we observe proper boundaries between our interests and others', something which won't be possible unless we can contain our desires and ambitions within the appropriate limits; this is the virtue of moderation or self-control. From the Stoic point of view, all of these virtues demand knowledge of what is good and bad. Courage, for instance, wouldn't be an excellence if it consisted in stubbornly standing by a misguided judgement that it is appropriate to die fighting on behalf of a cruel and undemocratic regime. Self-control couldn't be excellent unless I understood the *proper* limits of my desires for food, drink, and sexual fulfilment. There is, thus, a kind of unity among all the virtues (though Stoics could differ among themselves about how strong a unity it is), since they all consist at least partially in understanding what is good and bad, and being able to apply that understanding to the particular situations of life. (Box 10 illustrates this with a couple of passages from Epictetus.) These four virtues don't exhaust Stoic views on the topic, not least because they recognized that each of them can be further divided into more specific virtues depending on the circumstances in which we are called upon to act. Generosity, for example, is one form of justice and it is the applicable virtue when we are in certain situations of social privilege.

Box 10 Epictetus, *Discourse*

Basic conceptions are common to all people. And one basic conception does not conflict with another. For who among us does not hold that the good is advantageous and to be chosen and that we should go after it and pursue it in every circumstance? And who among us does not hold that the just is noble and fitting? So when does the conflict arise? It arises from the way basic conceptions are applied to particular substances, when one person says, 'He did well; he's a brave man', and another says, 'no, he's a madman.' That's the source of mutual conflict among people. This is the nature of the conflict between Jews and Syrians and Egyptians and Romans; it's not about whether one must honour what is holy above all else and pursue it always, but about whether eating this bit of pig flesh is holy or unholy. You will find that this was the source of conflict between Agamemnon and Achilles. Summon them here. Agamemnon, what do you say, shouldn't what is right and noble be brought about? 'Of course.' And what do you say, Achilles? Aren't you pleased when what is noble is brought about? 'That pleases me most of all.' Now apply the basic conceptions. That's where the conflict begins. One of them says, 'I do not have to give Chryseis back to her father', and the other says, 'yes, you must.' Certainly, one of them is misapplying the basic conception of obligation. Again, one of them says, 'therefore, if I must give Chryseis back I must also take a prize away from one of you', and the other says, 'Are you proposing to take the woman I love?' And the other says, 'yes, yours.' 'Am I then to be the only one...?' 'Then shall I be the only one not to have a prize?' That's how a conflict gets going.

So what is it to be getting educated? It's a matter of learning to apply the natural basic conceptions to particular substances in a manner that accords with nature... (1.22.1–9)

The starting point of philosophy, at least for those who approach it as they should, that is, through the front door, is an awareness of one's own weakness and incapacity when it comes to the necessities. We don't arrive possessing a natural notion of a right-angle triangle or a semitone interval; rather, we learn each of these by technical instruction; for this reason, those who don't know such things don't think they do. But who hasn't arrived possessing a natural notion of good, bad, noble, shameful, fitting and unfitting, happiness, suitable and incumbent, and of what one has to do and not do? That is why we all employ these words and try to apply our basic conceptions to particular substances. He did well, properly, not properly; he was unfortunate, he was fortunate; he is unjust, he is just. Who among us is stingy about using these words? Who among us defers using them until he learns them, like those who are ignorant about lines and sounds? The reason for this is that we arrive having already been taught by nature certain things in this area, and starting from those things we have added our own opinions as well. 'By Zeus, don't I know by nature what is noble and shameful? Don't I have a notion of it?' You do. 'And don't I apply it to particulars?' You do. 'And don't I apply it well?' This is the whole question, and here is where opinions get added in. For owing to inapposite application they start from these agreed points and proceed to what is debatable. What would stop them from being perfect if they had this [the ability to apply

(Continued)

Box 10 Continued

conceptions properly] in addition to those starting points? But now, since you think that you are also applying basic conceptions to particulars appositely, tell me, where did you get this ability? 'It's because I think it.' But this is exactly what someone else does not think, and he thinks that he is applying basic conceptions well. Doesn't he? 'He does.' Can you, then, both be applying basic conceptions appositely on matters where you hold conflicting views? 'No, we cannot.' So can you point to anything higher than your own opinion supporting your claim to apply basic conceptions better than he does? Does a madman do anything except what he thinks is noble? And is this criterion enough for him? 'No, it isn't.' Proceed on, then, to something higher than just opinion. 'What is this?' Behold! This is where philosophy begins ... (2.11.1–13)

It would take us too far afield to explore the highly ramified categories of the virtues—indeed, not all Stoics thought it was worthwhile to indulge in this kind of classificatory exercise. Instead, let's consider another very important approach to virtue and the best human life which is rooted in human nature. From this point of view, a rational, human life consists in a sequence of decisions to act; as long as we are doing things we have to decide what to do, and from Zeno onwards the Stoics put this issue in terms of determining what is the appropriate (*kathēkon*—the term is Zeno's coinage) thing to do. This is very much an intellectual exercise, demanding that we have a solid grasp of human nature, both general human nature and our own personal characteristics, our place in our society and in the cosmos, and clear insight into the relevant immediate circumstances. Cicero, again basing himself on the work of Panaetius, illustrates an important aspect of this kind of reasoning in Box 11.

Box 11 Cicero, *On Duties*

We should understand that we humans have been dressed, as it were, by nature for two roles. One of these is common to us all and derives from the fact that we all participate in rationality and the excellence which makes us superior to the beasts; this is the source of everything honourable and fitting, and the source of the reasoning we use in finding out what our responsibilities are. The other role is assigned separately to each of us. For just as there are great differences among our bodily attributes—we see that some people have swiftness suitable for running, others have the strength to be wrestlers, and similarly some people have dignified figures while others have graceful ones—so too there is an even greater variety in our mental makeup... (1.107)

To the two roles which I listed above a third is added, the role which certain chance circumstances force on us; and there is a fourth which we by our own decision adopt for ourselves. For kingdoms, military commands, high rank, civic honours, wealth, prosperity, and their opposites depend on chance and are governed by circumstances. But the role which we ourselves want to play comes from our choice. And so some people devote themselves to philosophy, others to civil law, others to public speaking and different people prefer to excel in different virtues. (1.115)

Whenever we are called upon to act we need to figure out the appropriate thing to do. If we were able to do so with perfect expertise then we would be virtuous agents and our actions would be more than just appropriate; they would be what the Stoics call 'perfectly appropriate actions' or 'right actions' (*katorthōmata*). But perfection is quite hard to achieve, and the Stoics were certainly right to concede that virtually no one ever makes it.

Someone who did so, however, would be an ideal to emulate, a paragon whose knowledge and ability to apply it to life represent the perfection of human nature and its rationality. For inspirational purposes the Stoics often talked about what this sort of wisdom would be like, all the while acknowledging that perhaps only one or two humans had ever achieved it (Socrates, certainly, and also Heracles—though the demi-god and son of Zeus perhaps had an unfair advantage over ordinary humanity). The Stoics invested a fair bit of effort in describing what such a perfectly wise person (or 'sage') would be like and in denying that anyone who falls short of that standard is really virtuous (on the grounds that virtue is a perfection and perfection does not come in degrees). The purpose of doing so can only have been protreptic and educational, encouraging us to self-improvement and establishing a target for anyone who is working towards becoming a better person and so ultimately achieving the goal of human life, which the Stoics identified with 'happiness' (*eudaimonia*).

Let's return to the issue of determining what is good and what is bad. Just as the Stoics took an unusually demanding position on the standards for virtue and wisdom, they also developed a very stringent and indeed counter-intuitive position on values. Following up on a line of argument found in some Socratic dialogues (*Gorgias* 467–468, *Euthydemus* 278–282, *Meno* 87–89; Xenophon, *Memorabilia* 4.6.8), the Stoics restricted the term 'good' to virtue and things that participate in it (like virtuous people); conversely, only vice and things that participate in it are bad. The reason given for this is simply that good is to be understood in very concrete terms as something which benefits its possessor and does so reliably. According to Socrates (and the Stoics were fully persuaded by this argument), only virtue can be counted on to benefit unconditionally and only vice counts as harmful in all possible circumstances. Other positive or appealing things, such as wealth, can in principle bring harm if they are misused, and sometimes even negative things that we ought normally to avoid can be good for us if they are handled properly. In both the positive and the negative case, the decisive role is played by the way circumstances are used, and the capacity for truly and consistently beneficial use of this sort of thing is the excellence we have been calling virtue.

This narrow Stoic conception of what is good and bad struck their contemporaries as deeply implausible. If, their critics sometimes argued, health and wealth are not good, why do we pursue them? Or was the Stoic point that we needn't bother doing so? (In that case, how could they claim to be advocating a life according to nature?) Either way, the picture of human nature and motivation offered by the Stoics begins to seem deeply unrealistic. Since the Stoics agreed with other ancient philosophers that ethics should at least be constrained by what is according to nature, they seemed to be vulnerable to decisive critique and rejection. How did they respond?

Certainly not by backing down from their Socratically based idealism. They stuck by the notion that virtue is the only reliably beneficial thing and so the only good, but they had no trouble at all in recognizing that there is another kind of value. Everything except virtue and vice was classified as indifferent (i.e. neither good nor bad). But some of these things are positive and naturally motivate us to pursue them and try to retain them (health and wealth, for example); others are negative and we naturally try to avoid them or eliminate them from our lives (disease and poverty, for example). It is part of human nature, as it is for any other living thing, to try to acquire the positive and to avoid the negative; clearly such things contribute to the normal and healthy life for an animal of our species; but the fact that they are not reliably beneficial and can be misused means that they do not qualify as good under the demanding Socratic standard adopted by the Stoics. The positive indifferents are labelled as 'preferred' and the negative ones 'dispreferred' or 'rejected'. (It's trivial but worth mentioning in passing that some indifferents are of no consequence for our lives—such as whether the number of stars in the sky or hairs on our head is odd or even. Things like that are labelled 'absolutely indifferent'. They can be ignored from here on in.)

Preferred indifferents have a kind of real value for us and dispreferred indifferents have a kind of real 'disvalue' (to emulate the Stoic neologism), but this sort of value is so different from the value of virtue and disvalue of vice that we must recognize a kind of dualism in their value theory. And indeed, the Stoics themselves argued vociferously that these two different scales of value are incommensurable with each other. If one were doing a calculus of value, in an effort to decide what the appropriate thing to do might be in a given situation, then no amount of any indifferent could outweigh the impact of what is truly good or bad (a virtuous or vicious action). Ideally one could live one's natural life as a human being (striving for health, wealth, good social relations, etc.) without it coming into conflict with our far more important aspiration to virtue and happiness; but if circumstances force a choice, then when it comes to deciding on the appropriate thing to do virtue wins every time.

The overriding value of virtue and vice when compared with indifferents is the most important message of Stoic ethics. As long as virtue and vice are not on the line, the wise agent will always strive for a better balance of preferred over dispreferred things, and the effort to achieve that is rational and natural behaviour: we are living according to nature in at least one sense: our human nature defines for us what things count as preferred and dispreferred. But if it ever becomes clear that virtue demands the sacrifice of preferred things then that is the way to go. And it is not just that doing the right thing (such as risking one's life to rescue someone or to preserve the state or forgoing profit for the sake of justice) can demand this sort of sacrifice. Since the overall plan of the cosmos is held to be an expression of the benevolent and perfect rationality of Zeus or Nature, any providential inevitability also warrants our deference. Whenever we act in accordance with our reason and the alignment with

Box 12 Epictetus, *Discourse*

If you always bear in mind what belongs to you and what belongs to others you will never be upset. This is why Chrysippus was right to say, 'As long as what comes next is unclear to me I will cling to what is more likely to lead to getting things in accordance with nature. For god made me such as to select those things. But if I did know that it is now fated for me to get sick, then I would even pursue that. In fact, one's foot, if it had intelligence, would pursue being muddied.' (2.6.8–10)

cosmic Nature that accompanies reason, then we are also living in accordance with Nature, this time in a much more comprehensive and authoritative sense. Chrysippus (Box 12) was very clear about the way the divine plan overrides our efforts to do what would otherwise be the natural thing, though it is important to emphasize once again how difficult it can be actually to know in advance what the will of Zeus (as it was often called) is. Surely, most of our concrete decisions about appropriate actions are decisively conditioned by our uncertainty about what Providence has in store for us—an uncertainty that makes it possible for us to strive in good faith for the 'good' (that is, naturally preferred) things in life. Unsurprisingly, their opponents did not take much notice of this nuanced position and focused most of their polemic on the more paradoxical aspects of Stoic ethics.

Human beings are by nature motivated to pursue happiness, their natural goal (*telos*), but they also have a motivation to pursue other values, though these lesser aims are always to be sacrificed if necessary. What, we might join their ancient opponents in asking, is the relationship between these two kinds of aim? We get some insight into this question by considering the variety of ways in which the Stoics described the *telos*, the goal of human life; a partial list of those ways is given in Box 13. Although the basic idea they were driving at did not change significantly over time, the various formulations of the *telos* tell us a lot about the development of the school.

Box 13 Stoic formulations of the *telos* (goal of life)

ZENO: to live in agreement [or, in agreement with nature—both versions are given] i.e. to live according to virtue

CLEANTHES: to live in agreement with nature

CHRYSIPPUS: to live according to the experience of the things which happen by nature

DIOGENES OF BABYLON: reasoning well in the selection and rejection of natural things

ARCHEDEMUS: to live completing all the appropriate acts

ARCHEDEMUS: to live selecting the most important and significant natural things, not being able to omit them

ANTIPATER: to live invariably selecting natural things and rejecting unnatural things

ANTIPATER: invariably and unswervingly to do everything in one's power for the attainment of the principal natural things.

PANAETIUS: to live according to the inclinations given to us by nature

POSIDONIUS: to live contemplating the truth and order of the universe and helping to construct that order as far as possible, not being dragged around by the irrational part of the soul in any respect

CERTAIN LATER STOICS: to live in agreement with the constitution of human beings.

We are told that some Stoics were particular about distinguishing human nature from the Nature of the cosmos (Diogenes, *Laërtius* 7.88); but there is another ambiguity in the term 'natural' or 'according to nature'. Sometimes, as when it refers to the Nature of the cosmos, it refers to what is demanded by the perfect rationality of the divine order in the natural world; but at other times it picks out what is in accordance with the preferred indifferents—the things that human nature will pursue providing that they fit in with the plan of Nature. We see this 'lower' sense of naturalness in the formulations of Archedemus and Antipater in Box 13 and it is further suggested by the references to our natural inclinations in Panaetius' formulation. It makes sense to take account of these natural inclinations, since it is uncontroversial that the pursuit of health and prosperity is natural for human beings, even when Nature's plan might be for some of us to die young or to be impoverished.

In order to accuse them of incoherence, critics of Stoic ethics in the ancient world took full advantage of the way Stoics described the *telos*, of having in effect two distinct and sometimes conflicting supreme goals. One was allegedly the successful achievement of the most important objects of our appropriate striving and desire, the preferred indifferents; and the other was the pursuit of happiness and virtue, a state of harmony with Nature that makes actually obtaining preferred indifferents irrelevant to our success. But though some Stoics may well have been guilty of sloppy expression, the criticism ultimately has no substance. It vaporizes once we take proper account of the fact that human beings are supposed to strive to attain preferred indifferents, the things that accord with our basic inclinations as members of our species, and at the same time must recognize that they are not the substance of happiness and that we need to let go of them with equanimity when we learn that achieving them is not part of the divine master plan. Pursuing material prosperity, for example, is natural and normal, and we should all do so, each in our own way. But we have to recognize that it is not the key to happiness, and this project should never be allowed to impinge on our much more important plan to achieve virtue; we should be ready at all times to abandon with a good grace our efforts to get rich when it appears that this is not what Zeus has in mind for us. The only thing we should be pursuing with unconditional commitment is virtue, for it is the only good and so the only thing that can make us happy.

We'll end this discussion of Stoic ethics with a brief look at one of their most paradoxical-sounding doctrines: the fully rational and wise person will be free of passions. There is a stereotype of Stoicism familiar to everyone, the claim that Stoicism involves being relentlessly rational, but without a trace of emotion— Mr Spock from Star Trek, only more so. That this isn't the right view of Stoicism is now generally understood, and specialists will even point out that the passions (*pathē*) from which the Stoic wise person is said to be free are not what we mean by emotions but a more narrowly defined group of states of mind that are by definition pathological. The wise person may well be perfectly rational, but that doesn't deprive him or her of all affective or emotional experience. He or she will feel 'joy' in the presence of good things and a form of 'wanting' to acquire them; similarly, there is a balanced and reasonable feeling of 'avoidance' at the prospect of bad things, such as vice and vicious people. These positive affective states stand in the place of the bad and misguided affective states characteristic of the non-wise. When what we are enjoying isn't a true good but something else, then we don't feel joy but mere 'pleasure', one of the four basic kinds of passion. Our striving to attain such pseudo-goods is what Stoics (and others) call 'desire' (*epithumia*), a disruptive and disturbing condition to be in. While the wise will avoid vice with a calm and steady affect, the foolish have the passion of 'fear', which accompanies or constitutes our attempts to avoid things that aren't really bad but are thought to be so. We fools may try to avoid vice, but we fear death (which is merely a dispreferred indifferent). The non-wise are also subject to another passion, for which there is no counterpart among the wise. 'Grief' or deep emotional pain (*lupē*) is what the foolish feel when they are in the grip of what they take to be bad states or conditions (such as loss of one's friends or family). The wise, however, are never in the grip of actual bad states—which could only be vice—so they don't have a counterpart of this passion. Instead, being always in a state of virtue (the good), their affective life is one of constant joy and tranquillity (even in dispreferred circumstances).

Two of these passions, pleasure and pain, are described with ambiguous terms, words that pick out either a purely physical condition or a cognitive and emotional state. The wise person is free of irrational and confused affects, but it is no part of Stoic doctrine to claim that the wise are free of physical pain and pleasure. They certainly suffer when their flesh is cut or burned, and feel pleasure when it is stimulated in the appropriate ways. But these physical states aren't vicious passions; they are merely indifferents, dispreferred and preferred, respectively.

The Stoic claim that the wise are free from the passions doesn't make them superhuman, nor does it make them apathetic zombies. Rather, they are pretty much what we would expect them to be: completely reasonable people who assess all of their own experience by the standards of reason. The wise man will love his wife and take pleasure in her company, but will recognize that any human being is mortal and so not a reliable source of goodness. If his wife is wise too, then her virtue will bring him joy as a part of his happy state of mind. But if not, there is still satisfaction in their relationship and a genuine human attachment. If she dies, though, will he not suffer grief (*lupē*)? No, and that is where the Stoic's freedom from passion really comes into play. We can look at this issue through the eyes of the later Stoic, Epictetus. (See Box 14.) In his version of this Stoic doctrine, the wise person will never strive for or aim unconditionally to retain anything that could not be reliably secured by his or her own efforts—and that is the improvement of his or her own character and intellectual condition. Things like wealth, a loving

Box 14 Epictetus, *Handbook*

> With everything that charms you or is useful to you or
> that you cherish, remember to say what it is really like,
> starting with the smallest things. If you cherish a jug,
> say 'I cherish a jug.' For when it breaks you will not be
> disturbed. If you are caressing your child or your wife, say
> that you are caressing a human being. For when they die
> you will not be disturbed. (3)

partner, and children are subject to the apparent vagaries of fate.
If someone were to aim at that sort of thing, thinking of them as
being 'good', then he or she would in fact be devastated at their
loss. (Similarly, *mutatis mutandis*, for things he or she might
avoid, thinking of them as being genuinely bad.)

In Epictetus' view, trying to get or keep indifferents as though
they are good is a recipe for misery, and trying to avoid or
eliminate indifferents as though they are bad is the same. Instead,
he recommends, we should begin from a proper understanding
of what is genuinely good (virtue) and bad (vice) and only direct
our vigorous and zealous efforts at those things. (Epictetus is
particularly emphatic about the fundamental difference between
what is 'up to us' and what is 'not up to us', that is, things either
subject to our deliberate choice and effort (*prohairesis*) or not.)
If we do that then we won't ever have to suffer the dreadful
emotions properly called passions. Of course, Epictetus is
perfectly clear that we can try to get or avoid indifferents and
naturally have a certain reaction to our successes and failures in
such endeavours. But all such efforts have to be tempered by the
realization that what is at stake is not a matter of happiness or
misery and that success is never to be taken for granted. His
recommendation is to pursue such things with a light touch, a
kind of mental reservation that already anticipates the prospect
of failure or reversal. Stoics also advised us to prepare for things

turning out badly by actually imagining misfortune (such as the death of a child) striking us, so that when and if such a thing happens it does not catch us unprepared. This was called the 'pre-rehearsal of bad outcomes' (*praemeditatio malorum*) and was also adopted by some other schools of philosophy as a practical expedient. For Stoics, however, it was based on the sharp distinction between good/bad on the one hand and preferred/dispreferred on the other.

Prepared in these ways for disappointment, the wise person will never feel the unreliable pleasure of seeming to attain a good that is no such thing, never suffer grief at the loss of something that is actually vital for human happiness, nor will he or she suffer the turmoil of passionate desire or panicky fear. Instead, knowing the true value of things (which is the core of wisdom for the Stoics) the wise person will be reasonable in his or her efforts to get or avoid indifferent things and equally reasonable in reacting to success or failure. Even someone who is not yet wise, but is merely working to develop these attitudes, will benefit from this kind of affective reasonableness, while still, of course, being vulnerable to mistakes and relapses. It is only when all such appropriate actions produce absolutely reliable and solid habits, so that the actions are perfectly correct (*katorthōmata*), that wisdom can be recognized and the experience of pure joy at a genuinely and reliably good state of affairs (virtue) can be savoured

Chapter 6
Logic

The Stoic teacher Epictetus organized a good deal of his thinking about rationality around the idea of 'using impressions'. An impression (*phantasia*) is the basic unit of mental activity for Stoics, but the term itself goes back to Plato, who used it to refer to the way things *look* to us, and to Aristotle, who made great progress in turning it into a technical term in psychology. The Stoics went further down this road. A *phantasia* is first and foremost the change in the mind of any animal brought about by its perceptual interaction with the outside world. Material objects cause changes in the medium between themselves and the sense organs, and those changes cause further changes in the senses, which then get propagated through the animal's sensory system to its 'mind' or central coordinating part (its 'leading part' or 'principle' (*hēgemonikon*), consisting of suitably qualified *pneuma*). There such changes register as perceptions, changes which inform the animal about the object that was the ultimate origin of this chain of material causal interactions. Though things can go wrong with this sort of causal chain, Nature has designed the system to succeed in the standard case. That is, in the normal case animals successfully rely on the accuracy of their perceptions to enable them to get around in the world and carry out their characteristic functions. A rational, providential force like Nature doesn't set its creatures up for failure; there is no evil demon systematically deceiving them about what is the case in the world.

Human animals, though, are rational and for them the system just described is more complicated. When we receive impressions from the outside world we have a special kind of awareness of it; rational animals receive impressions as *rational* impressions, which means that there is a sayable content (a *lekton*) associated with them. Those contents are things which we are aware of and though incorporeals cannot actually cause anything their presence makes it possible for rational animals to assess impressions and so to make use of them in various ways. One of the most important things we can do with our impressions is to decide whether or not to accept them as reliable. Imagine getting the impression of a snake lying in a darkened room. My dog (who is as frightened of snakes as I am) backs out of the room, growling and with his tail between his legs, a virtually automatic and obviously adaptive reaction (Nature is looking out for Rover by making him cautious about potential threats). But unlike Rover I have a self-conscious understanding of the impression I am getting. I can, in effect, say to myself, 'hang on a minute; is this a real snake or a harmless coil of rope glimpsed in bad light?' I can then decide, on reflection, that it's a misleading impression and can reject it—'get back in here, Rover, you silly dog; it's just a bit of old rope.' Or maybe Rover's instinctive response was right and it really is a dangerous snake. I then give it my assent and join him cowering in the next room as I nervously ring up the animal control people.

The ability to give or withhold assent to an impression is the fundamental power that our rationality gives us for dealing with the outside world; for the Stoics it is what makes us reflective, critical, and so rational animals. Without the access to the intelligible content in the world made possible by our special minds (special by comparison with other animals) we would be automatic parts of a causal chain just like those animals. With it, we of course remain parts of the causal chain (even our assent is a physical event in our physical mind) but we possess an internal switch, as it were, that serves to make our internal mental activity a decisive node in the causal chain: depending on what we do in response to impressions from the outside world, things will go this way (if we assent) or that way (if we don't). By now we know that the way we respond is also determined by a causal setup (our minds are what they are because of prior causes and this structures our responses), but luckily we cannot be aware of that setup so we make our choices as 'free' agents.

But that's not all that we can do with our impressions. They are also the basis for our general concepts of things and we can learn to process and manipulate them (with their associated contents, of course); the process is illustrated in Box 15. This sort of internal management of contentful impressions is what makes rational animals genuinely rational, thinking entities—and this in broad outline is the cognitive psychology developed by Stoicism. Their philosophical opponents, some of whom were deeply committed to the idea that thought is essentially an incorporeal

Box 15 Aëtius

The Stoics say: when a human being is born the leading part of his soul is like a sheet of paper prepared for being written upon. And on it are written each and every one of our conceptions.

The first form of writing is through the senses. For when we have perceived something, for example a white thing, when it is gone we retain a memory of it. When we have many memories of the same kind then we say we have experience of it, a set of many impressions of the same kind is experience.

Of conceptions, some occur naturally in the ways indicated and without technical development but others occur directly through teaching and practice. The latter are called just conceptions, while the former are also called 'basic conceptions'. (4.11.1–5)

activity, rejected their analysis; but since thinking is causally efficacious the Stoics were constrained by their status as Giants to provide a corporealist account of the workings of the mind. Their story about incorporeal mental content accompanying such workings is an essential part of that theory. Materialist and scientific theories of how the mind operates are, of course, still with us today; this kind of debate about the material basis of thought (whether it be neurons or the Stoics' counterpart, *pneuma*) and its relationship with the content and meaning which form the substance of our mental awareness is still one that provokes disagreement. For what it's worth, the Stoics turn out to have been pioneers in one of the longest-running and still unresolved debates in the history of philosophy.

Let's go back to Epictetus (see Box 7 again). His focus on the 'use of impressions' as the key to our mental life is standard Stoic theory, but his terminology for this doctrine is very much his own. When he says that this 'use' is what makes us self-aware, critical animals, able to analyse the world and decide on our own path through life, he is really talking about impressions as the bearers of this kind of content. Whether or not we accept the Stoic way of handling the challenge of accounting for cognitive activity in a materialist framework, it can be recognized as the foundation of a critically important part of their overall philosophy. If, like most Platonists in antiquity, we reject this 'metaphysics of the mind' and insist that thinking is an exclusively incorporeal activity, then a great deal of what is distinctive about Stoicism has to be rejected—and this is, I think, pretty much what happened in later antiquity, leading to the collapse of the Stoic project and the absorption of its remnants into Platonism.

Logic has a broad and a narrow sense in Stoic theory. We have been talking so far about some features of the broad sense, the study of what makes us rational—logic (the Stoic *logikē*) as the theory of *logos*. But there is a more specific and technical sense of 'logic' in the ancient world, one that aligns well with what we tend to mean by the term today. And that is the narrowly focused study of forms of inference, validity, argumentation, and so forth. The Stoics were great pioneers in this study as well (it was one of Chrysippus' claims to fame) and active research in logic in this specialized sense was a part of Stoic thought from beginning to end. The broad and narrow senses of logic were closely connected. For logical relations were held to be relations among contents (the sayables) as abstracted from their material hosts. Complementing their account of sayables as one of the four kinds of incorporeal somethings, the Stoics distinguished *signifiers* (*sēmainonta*) from *things signified* or meanings (*sēmainomena*). Meanings are incorporeal sayables, while the study of signifiers was an investigation into the physical basis of communication (sounds, words, grammatical analysis, etc.)—essentially laying the foundations for linguistics alongside logic and the philosophy of language.

Logic in the narrower technical sense deals with a subset of sayables and meanings. What the Stoics called 'complete' sayables are *axiōmata*, something very close to what we now mean by propositions. An *axiōma* is content that is either true or false (unlike the content of a wish or a command, for instance) and the relationships among such things (which, for convenience, we may as well call propositions) are the stuff and substance of logical relationships. Their logic, then, is close to what we would call propositional logic, in contrast to classic Aristotelian logic, for which the basic units whose formal relationships are analysed are *terms* predicated of one another in various ways. When propositions become the basic unit of analysis, we get a form of logic whose centrality was pioneered by the Stoics, forgotten or neglected for centuries, and then revived in the modern era to become the backbone of logical study today.

We have only fragments of the logical theory of Chrysippus—he was certainly the pioneer and genius of Stoic logic, though many others made important contributions in later generations. But what we do have reveals a vital interest in logical foundations. Chrysippus seems to have held that in simple assertoric logic (as opposed to modal logic, for example, which he also studied at great length) all valid inference forms could be reduced to combinations of five basic and indemonstrable argument forms, with the assistance of several other logical and metalogical principles. Box 16 sets out these indemonstrables. We should note here the Stoic use of 'variables' ('the first', 'the second', etc.) which stand for propositions rather than terms, as in Aristotelian logic ('all A is B', etc.).

Box 16 The Stoic indemonstrables

I
If the first, the second.
But the first.
∴ the second.

II
If the first, the second.
But not the second.
∴ not the first.

III
Not both the first and the second.
But the first.
∴ not the second.

IV
Either the first or the second.
But the first.
∴ not the second.

V
Either the first or the second.
But not the second.
∴ the first.

The Stoics did not limit themselves to such straightforward analysis, but also worked extensively on modal syllogistic and other areas of research in logic with a sophistication not paralleled in some cases until the 20th century. The Stoics also undertook a comprehensive study of other non-assertoric sentence forms, of various logical puzzles and their solutions, and of paradoxes such as the Liar, according to which when someone says, 'I am lying', we cannot determine whether it is a true or false statement. Other logicians in antiquity (such as Aristotle and his followers) had tackled this kind of problem case, but the Stoics stood head and shoulders above others as specialists in logical puzzles and problems—so much so that it provoked a reaction among later Stoics, such as Seneca and Epictetus, who objected to the amount of energy poured into this part of philosophy; they thought, perhaps rightly, that it distracted attention from the more important parts of philosophy: physics and ethics, and their practical application to life. Despite that protest (with which some of our contemporaries might sympathize after considering the attention devoted to some highly technical areas of philosophical research), Epictetus and Seneca both clearly understood Stoic logic well and Epictetus was an accomplished teacher of the subject. It has to be said, though, that enthusiasm for technical logic was very much a specialized 'in-school' sort of thing and other followers of the school, such as Marcus Aurelius, were inclined to reject logic altogether as being not worth the time; in this they were following up on a trend that developed early in the school's history, with Aristo of Chios, one of Zeno's first students.

Despite the occasional impatience of some Stoics, it's worth looking at some of the key developments in Stoic logic, especially ones that interact with other parts of their philosophy. One such issue arises from their analysis of modal concepts (possibility, necessity, and so forth), a subject interesting in its own right and intimately connected with the Stoic worries about determinism (see Chapter 4). As far as we can tell, the key developments in this area did not come from the founder, Zeno, but from Chrysippus (whose extensive bibliography includes at least a hundred titles dealing with various logical topics). It says a good deal about the way philosophy developed in the Hellenistic period that Chrysippus' theories in this department did not emerge as a *direct* reaction to Plato or even Aristotle. Rather, it was primarily a reaction to the challenging theories put forward in the late 4th and early 3rd centuries BCE by a group of philosophers interested in a variety of philosophical problems dealing with modality, semantics, and dialectic. At least some of these philosophers were pursuing the kind of problems about determinism that already worried Aristotle in his discussion of future contingent propositions in *On Interpretation*. The famous example is 'there will be a sea battle tomorrow', a claim that isn't necessary in the way of eternal truths, such as a prediction that 'horses will have four legs tomorrow' or 'triangles will be plane figures bounded by three straight lines tomorrow'. The ancients were generally confident that the last two predictions were necessarily true, and no one worried about determinism as a result. But when it comes to predicting contingent events, like sea battles, things are different. If the future claim is true, the worry is that it is already fixed and necessary (in which case all diplomatic efforts to avoid the battle are pointless); if it isn't true, the worry is that the non-occurrence of the battle is also necessary (in which case there is no need to bother with diplomacy, since the false prediction is just a false alarm). But if it is neither true nor false, then a basic logical law seems to be broken (that all well-formed propositions are either true or false). We should note that the Stoics also faced this kind of critique against their determinism (the argument was called 'the Lazy Argument') and their response to it rested on what was called the doctrine of 'co-fated events': if it is fated that the sea battle be averted, then the negotiations which lead to that outcome are also fated, being so tightly connected causally that the one could not occur without the other.

The two most important members of this group of philosophers were Philo, from the city of Megara, and Diodorus Cronus—the former gave the group its usual label, 'the Megarians'. Addressing problems like the sea battle requires hard thinking about what terms like 'possible' and 'necessary' mean. Philo stepped up to the plate and proposed that the *possible* is a proposition that is capable of being true in its own nature and the *necessary* is a proposition that is true and in its own nature cannot be false; definitions of the *non-necessary* and the *impossible* followed from these. Diodorus also defined the modal concepts in terms of truth, but without relying on the notion that a proposition has some intrinsic suitability for truth or falsity. Rather, nothing but truth values is invoked in defining the basic modal notions. For Diodorus the *possible* is that which is or will be true; the *impossible* is that which is false and will not be true; the *necessary* is that which is true and will not be false; and the *non-necessary* is that which is false now or will be false.

There is something attractively economical about defining modal concepts solely in terms of truth and falsity, though we should note that in this ancient debate it is assumed that propositions can change their truth value: a single proposition ('Rover bites the mailman') is false today but will be true tomorrow. But Diodorus' approach brings worries about determinism to the fore: taken together they seem to entail that something that isn't going to happen isn't even possible, and that something that is going to happen is thereby necessary. If it is true that there isn't going to be a sea battle tomorrow then it's impossible that there will be one. And we are right back into the worries about determinism again: it turns out to be either necessary that there be a sea battle tomorrow (if it happens at all) or impossible (if it doesn't). Diodorus had a clever argument that he used to support his concepts of necessity and possibility, called the Master Argument (see Box 17). We are told by Epictetus that several Stoics, including Chrysippus, tried out different responses to it. It seems that debate about all of these

Box 17 Epictetus, *Discourse*

The Master Argument seems to have been advanced on the basis of starting points of this sort. These three claims are in general conflict with each other: (1) everything past and true is necessary; (2) what is impossible does not follow from what is possible; (3) what neither is nor will be true is possible. Seeing this conflict Diodorus employed the plausibility of the first two to establish the conclusion that nothing is possible that neither is nor will be true. But one person will retain this pair of propositions: that there is something possible that neither is nor will be true and that what is impossible does not follow from what is possible; they hold that not everything past and true is necessary. This seems to be the tendency of Cleanthes and his followers, who are greatly supported by Antipater. Others accept the other pair of propositions, that there is something possible which neither is nor will be true and that everything past and true is necessary; they hold that something impossible can follow from what is possible. But it is impossible to hold all three of these propositions owing to their general conflict.

If someone asks me, 'which pair do you hold?' I will reply to him, 'I don't know. But I have learned by research that Diodorus held one pair, Panthoides, Cleanthes, and their followers a different pair, and Chrysippus the remaining pair.' 'But what about you?' That's not what I was born for, to test my own impression and to compare what people say on the topic and to form an opinion of my own on the subject. For this reason I am no better than a grammarian. 'Who was Hector's father?' Priam. 'Who where his brothers?' Alexander and Deiphobus. 'Who was their mother?' Hecuba. This is what my research has taught me.

(Continued)

Box 17 Continued

'Who was your source?' Homer. But I think that
Hellanicus and maybe others like him write on the same
issues. And when it comes to the Master Argument,
what else do I have that's any better? But if I'm an empty
boaster I can wow people at a dinner party by counting
off those who have written about it. 'Chrysippus wrote
brilliantly on this in book one of his *On Possibility*. And
Cleanthes wrote a separate book on the problem and so
too did Archedemus. Antipater too wrote on it, not only
in his *On Possibility* but also separately in his book on the
Master Argument. Haven't you read it?' 'No, I haven't.'
'You must read it.' And how will that benefit him? He
will just be more of an importunate blatherer than he is
now. As for you, what else have you gotten out of
reading it? What opinion have you formed on the issue?
No, you'll tell us about Helen and Priam and Calypso's
island, that never existed nor will it! In this area it's not a
big deal if you master the research but don't make any
opinion your very own. But in ethics we fall prey to this
much more than in literature. 'Tell me about things
good and bad.' 'Listen: A wind from Troy carried me
near to the shore of the Ciconians [*Odyssey* 9.39]. Some
things are good, some bad, some indifferent. The good
things are virtues and what participates in them, the
bad things are vices and what participates in them, and
the indifferents are those in between, such as wealth,
health, life, death, pleasure, and pain.' Where did you
learn that? 'Hellanicus says it in his *Egyptian Tales*.' For
how is it any better to say this than to say that Diogenes
said it in his *Ethics* or Chrysippus or Cleanthes? Have you
put any of these things to the test and come to your
own view? Show me how you usually behave when your

> ship is storm-tossed? Do you remember this division when
> the sail is snapping and you are crying aloud, and some
> mischievous guy comes up to you and says, 'Tell me again,
> by the gods, what you were saying just now. Surely
> shipwreck is not a bad thing since it surely doesn't
> participate in vice.' Won't you seize a piece of wood and
> swing it at him? 'Hey you! What's it to you? We're going
> down and you come along and make jokes!' (2.19.1–16)

matters was particularly important to the Stoics because of their
own need to find a way to reconcile causal determinism with
the avoidance of the kind of necessity that would undermine a
recognition of human possibilities.

And so Chrysippus also proposed definitions of the key modal
concepts, using a logical challenge to support his physics and his
ethics. According to him, the *possible* is a proposition that is
capable of being true and is not prevented by external factors from
being true, and the *necessary* either is true and not capable of
being false, or is capable of being false but is prevented from being
false by external factors. Right away we can see that he has
re-introduced considerations besides the bare truth and falsity of
propositions to which Diodorus restricted himself, but that he has
nevertheless incorporated some features of Diodorus' theory.

Logic

Scholarly debate about the way Stoic modalities were meant to
work continues, of course. But for our purposes the most
interesting feature of their theory is the way it seems to connect to
their worries about determinism and compatibilism. Let's take the
situation of the famous Roman statesman Cicero, whose own
philosophy was Academic rather than Stoic. We know from his
correspondence (*Letters to Atticus* 16.7) that at a key point in the
civil war poor Cicero had debated and dithered about whether to
leave town or to stay and work for his political agenda in Rome;

after much anguished hand-wringing he decided to run for it, but was caught by his enemies anyway and executed. Let's imagine ourselves by his side as he deliberates what to do and consider from a Stoic point of view the proposition 'Cicero will leave Rome tomorrow.' It is a true proposition, which means that by Diodorus' definitions it is necessary. But by Chrysippus' definitions the prediction can be true without being necessary. Though Cicero's decision to flee is causally determined, like everything according to the Stoics, it is still possible rather than necessitated. To see how this works, remember how the Stoics explain human action. Our decisions are all caused, but each is caused by two factors: external considerations and one's own character. For Cicero, the external factors are clear: the growing power of his enemy Antonius and the consequent danger of immediate arrest and summary execution if he stays. That's the external stimulus (an impression of imminent danger) that stimulates his flight. But the other factor is his own character, an internal cause of his ultimate decision to flee; Cicero's patriotism inclined him to try to live to fight for his beloved Republic another day, but his bad judgement led him to believe that his plans might succeed. Chrysippus' definition of the possible reflects this situation. The possible is what is capable of being true and is not prevented from being true by *external* factors. Cicero's flight is capable of being true—it is a choice within his power to make; and it isn't prevented from happening by anything external (such as being arrested and imprisoned before he even left his house). We can see that Cicero's ultimately futile flight was determined but not necessitated—the alternative was possible, under Chrysippus' definition. How was the alternative possible? The only thing that could have prevented it from taking place was something *internal*, his own character and temperament.

Here we see a clear example of logic being integrated with physics and ethics. The causal account of Cicero's escape is deterministic, as required by Stoic physics, and we can see that the doctrine of fate is illustrated by it—there is an external stimulus interacting with internal factors, such as Cicero's character. The ethical significance of Cicero's decision is clear, in that he made a real choice whether to go or to stay, based on his values, his assessment of the situation, and his deliberative capacity. He hesitated—rather, he *deliberated* about what to do; and he was responsible for his decision. An omniscient observer could certainly have predicted how the deliberation would end, but Cicero himself could not; he didn't have the kind of thorough self-knowledge that would have led him to predict his own behaviour (a hypothetical self-awareness which may well have paralysed him). None of this would be defensible as an account of Cicero's actions if a critic could successfully claim that his flight was necessitated, but it is precisely the revision to the notion of the possible that blocks this move by a critic. As we have seen, logic is treated by the Stoics as something more than a subject of specialized interest to experts; it is also a defensive wall around the core doctrines of physics and ethics. It is their logic which enables Stoics to defend their account of Cicero's action in response to a moral dilemma as being determined but not necessitated. It's a subtle point, but a classic example of Stoic logic at work.

Another illustration of Stoic logic being put to work for systematic purposes can be found if we focus for a moment on one of the favourite words of any logician, 'if'. Sentences connected by 'if…then' are called conditionals and different systems of logic have different ways of interpreting the conditional. As with their modal concepts, the Stoic approach to conditionals needs to be considered against the background of Megarian logical theories. Philo and Diodorus both proposed conditionals that we would classify as 'truth-functional'. That is, in a condition such as 'if p then q' the truth of the conditional is determined solely by the truth of the two component propositions, p and q. Philo held that such a conditional is false only when p is true and q is false; otherwise it is true, regardless of any other relationship between p and q. This has the odd result of making conditionals like 'if it is day I have blue eyes' true all day long—even though there is no logical or causal linkage between my eye colour and the position of the sun relative to the earth—and the even odder result that the conditional is true at night. For if 'it is day' is false then the conditional doesn't begin from a truth and end in a falsehood, which makes it true by Philo's lights.

Logicians will agree that there is nothing wrong with this sort of conditional (often called a material conditional) and even some real advantages from the point of view of doing logic. But if you want to use conditionals to understand actual connections in the world, as the Stoics did when doing physics or ethics, then the material conditional leaves something to be desired. The standard Stoic example of a conditional is 'if it is day it is light' and this illustrates the key difference between a Philonian conditional and a Stoic conditional. For Chrysippus (who was, we think, responsible for this bit of logical doctrine) there has to be a significant 'connection' (*sunartēsis*) between p and q; it is this connection, whether it is purely conceptual or empirically based, which legitimizes the use of 'if . . . then'. The connection between 'it is day' and 'it is light' is pretty obvious; it is the sort of thing that is missing from 'if it is day I have blue eyes'. But the notion of connection is still a bit informal, which won't do for a logician; so Chrysippus firmed things up by explaining the connection in terms of 'conflict' (*machē*). He seems to have said that a conditional such as 'if p then q' is true if p and not-q conflict with each other. There is a conflict between its being day and its not being light—you just never find both of these states of affairs obtaining together. But there is no such conflict between its being day and my eyes not being blue. If I had brown eyes, for instance, the sun would still rise tomorrow. There is simply no connection between my eye colour and the sun's position relative to the earth. So a Stoic conditional, unlike a Philonian conditional, is well-suited for making reliably meaningful claims about the relationships between things in the real world, including cosmological facts, physical facts, and facts in ethics: if you heat water it evaporates more quickly; if a person is virtuous she is happy.

The importance of such logical connections for expressing causal relationships of various sorts was so great that when their physical theory led them to doubt the presence of a proper causal connection between p and q they would scrupulously avoid using the conditional to express it. We learn from Cicero (*On Fate* 11–15), for example, that there were cases where a regular co-occurrence of events was observed but at least some Stoics doubted a direct causal connection. So in astrology (which was a proper physical science for ancient Stoics) Chrysippus did not want to say that 'if someone was born at the rising of the Dog Star he will not die at sea'. Chrysippus' worry here was that being born at a certain time is necessary once it has occurred and if the two facts are connected by a proper conditional then the necessity of the past would be passed on to the claim about the future. But (as we saw earlier) even causally determined predictions weren't supposed to be *necessary*, at least not all of them. So instead of using the conditional to express this relationship Chrysippus insisted on saying 'it is not the case both that someone was born at the rising of the Dog Star and that he will not die at sea'. The relationship is represented with a 'negated conjunction' rather than a conditional and since there is no connection (*sunartēsis*) of the relevant sort the necessity doesn't get passed along to the future.

This may seem like quibbling. After all, 'if p then q' with a Philonian, truth-functional sense of 'if' is equivalent to 'not both p and not-q'. So it might look as though Chrysippus is just playing with words to evade a problem for his theory—a criticism that Stoics often had to face (one critic called them 'word warriors' (Clement *Strom.* 2.7.33)), and the later Academic Antiochus accused the Stoics of innovating in words while in fact holding the same views as some other philosophers. But the difference between a Philonian 'if' and a Chrysippean 'if' isn't something cooked up just to solve this particular problem. The idea that 'if…then' indicates some sort of 'real' connection between two states of affairs or propositions is intuitive and much closer to natural language than Philo's revisionist understanding of 'if' as the material conditional. If someone is 'playing with words' to address some problem, then for once it won't be the Stoics! That said, Chrysippus' insistence on recasting the astrological prediction into truth-functional form (avoiding the use of 'if') does show him once again deploying logical theory in order to defend Stoic positions in physics and ethics. That doesn't, of course, mean that the logical theory isn't something to be taken seriously or that it isn't a genuine philosophical contribution. It just shows that those analogies used to illustrate the relationship among the three parts of philosophy really do tell us something about how Stoicism was meant to work.

Chapter 7
Stoicism, then and now

In the 21st century it would be hard to make the case that learning the details of ancient Stoic cosmology or mastering Chrysippus' syllogistic theory would be part of a plan for living a better life, for achieving happiness or balance or contentment. Such a study would be interesting for many people and intellectually rewarding, but not the key to living well in our day and age. And yet people still look to Stoicism for guidance and inspiration in achieving just such goals, and by all accounts it works for many of them. We began this *Very Short Introduction* with a reflection on the contrast between the contemporary reception of Stoicism and the academic study of the ancient school which remains its inspiration—and the gap between these two ways of engaging with the school founded by Zeno of Citium can seem enormous.

By looking at the history of Stoicism's influence since its rediscovery in the Renaissance we have seen one way that these two approaches can be brought into contact with each other: the prominence of Epictetus and Marcus Aurelius (and to a lesser degree Seneca) in the contemporary reception of Stoicism has made it natural to focus primarily on its potential as a source for moral advice and self-improvement. *Stoicism Today* and other such works, some bordering on the evangelical in their attitude, reflect in large measure the Stoicism of the Renaissance recovery, modern incarnations of the kind of cultural forces which have so frequently embraced and adapted the ancient originals. Since the Renaissance we have been able to do this only for those few works which chanced to survive from antiquity, and that has powerfully shaped our modern sense of what Stoicism can mean for us. The three major surviving Stoic authors have made the practical side of ethics and moral practice seem like the core of Stoic thought. Because of this focus, even when works of these authors do deal with physics (which is well-represented in Seneca's *Natural Questions*) or logic (an important theme in Epictetus, whose account of the Master Argument is a key source for our knowledge of Stoic modal theory) this fades into the background. Works produced in the current revival of Stoicism do not have sections on Chrysippus' syllogistic or the cosmic 'conflagration'.

Another way these two approaches can be connected is through reflection on the variety within the ancient school. As we have seen, Stoicism embraced two tendencies: Large Stoicism, which became the standard approach and aimed to integrate physics (including cosmology and theology) and logic with ethics; and Minimal Stoicism, which argued that all one needed was ethics. Minimal Stoicism is associated most strongly with Zeno's student, Aristo of Chios, but his influence continued to be felt right to the end of the school in antiquity (he was mentioned favourably by both Seneca and Marcus), while Large Stoicism represents the victory of Cleanthes and Chrysippus in the contest for the right to interpret the work of the founder. Modern Stoics aiming primarily to improve human lives through moral betterment, setting aside physics and logic, can see themselves as the heirs of Aristo's tradition, one that goes back to the early days of the school. It's not just our modern reliance on Marcus, Epictetus, and Seneca that feeds this movement; a narrow focus on ethical improvement is also an authentic component of ancient Stoicism.

But it's not the whole story, as we have seen, and the philosophers who insist that the goal of life, the aim of ethical improvement, is to live according to nature cannot ultimately ignore the study of nature. How else can we know what to follow? Nor can anyone aspiring to understand nature, or even to behave ethically in a rational way, ignore the study of reasoning, that is, logic. A modern Stoic, then, might well be missing something if they are too steadfastly devoted to Minimal Stoicism or to practical ethics alone. Here, then, there are interesting questions to ask about the relationship between our two ways of engaging with Stoicism. How much of ancient Stoic logic does the modern Stoic need? Arguably none, as long as they are dedicated to living a fully rational life and have embraced today's current best canons for reasoning as a guide and constraint. To the extent that Stoic logic played a supporting role in the ancient school we should be able to replace it with modern theories and practices of reasoning—as indeed many modern Stoics in practice do.

Things are more complicated, though, when we ask what we are to do about Stoic physics. Ancient Stoics, from Zeno to Marcus Aurelius, thought of ethical progress within the context of a natural philosophy that rested on a kind of cosmic holism, deterministic and providential, guided by a divine intelligence with which human beings need to align themselves. Stoic physics claimed that humans have access to a godlike rationality which mirrors the reason that runs the world, that as a species we are superior to everything else in nature, that all other animals exist to serve our interests. All of nature is made of four elements (earth, air, fire, and water) and consists of a unique and finite cosmos with our earth at the centre. And so on. Ancient Stoic physics, then, is clearly obsolete and no reasonable person can believe in it any more. Ancient Stoics, believing that the best life is a life according to nature, didn't just have human nature in mind; they aspired to live a life in accordance with the nature of the whole world as well, the world described by Stoic physics. Modern Stoics surely can't do that!

This, of course, is one reason why contemporary Stoics tend towards Minimal Stoicism; the life according to nature that Zeno,

Chrysippus, Seneca, and Marcus knew cannot be the life for us. As we think about the relationship between our two approaches to Stoicism, can we find any common ground here?

For the most part the answer has been 'no'. But even though Stoic physics as outlined in this *Introduction* is no fit guide for modern rational life, there is something very attractive about the idea of a Stoic life built around the constraints imposed by the world we live in. In 1998, the philosopher Lawrence Becker embarked on a bold thought experiment, publishing a book, *A New Stoicism*, that challenges us to rethink Stoicism for the modern world. The problem, as Becker so perceptively saw, is that the Stoicism of the ancient world stopped developing. Stoic science was once state-of-the-art (divinely providential teleology and all) and in those days it made perfect sense to say to rational people that they should live in accordance with nature—it just meant, as Becker, rephrasing the Stoic credo, put it, 'following the facts'. If the fulfilment of a rational human being is to be found in using our reason to understand the world and to navigate our way within that world, then many if not most of us could embrace that aim. The Stoic 'life according to nature' could still be with us after all; it's just that our modern conception of the natural world, our sense of what 'the facts' really are, has matured. Perhaps we don't have to abandon natural philosophy to connect with Stoicism today; perhaps we just have to live according to our current understanding of nature rather than the obsolete cosmology that gave such comfort to Marcus Aurelius.

But would the result still be Stoicism? Modern science ('the facts' we are to follow) has no place for providential teleology. Although we might retain determinism, we have to jettison the comforts of knowing that humans have a unique and special place in a world administered by a divine plan. We can no longer think of the world and its denizens as having been put here for our benefit. We live on a small planet circling a small star situated in a rather ordinary seeming galaxy, just one among billions. How could using our reason to live according to this understanding of nature have anything to do with Stoicism? Becker's book aims to answer this question, and there is no doubt about the outcome: Stoicism in the world of modern science is different—to see how it might differ you'll just have to read Becker's book (a revised edition came out in 2017). No summary here could do it justice, and his proposal is certainly not the only one possible.

Even if Stoicism for the modern world were significantly transformed by swapping out an obsolete understanding of the natural world for one based on our current best science, it would, I contend, still be worth doing. The intellectual attraction of ancient Stoicism as we've come to understand it in modern academic study lies above all in its integration, in its vision of a way of life rooted in the use of reason to navigate life and fulfil our nature as human beings, in the context of the best available understanding of our place in the world. Ancient Stoics believed, and so perhaps may some of us, that the good life is better to the extent that it encompasses everything that we can know about our place in the world. That, of course, is the vision of Large Stoicism, the vision of Cleanthes and Chrysippus, not of the Minimal Stoicism we discover in the philosophy of Aristo. Even for those of us who limit our exploration of Stoicism to Epictetus, Marcus, and Seneca, this should still be the vision that inspires. For despite their apparently lop-sided focus on ethics they were nevertheless all adherents of Large Stoicism, believers in the providentially organized world that passed for the best science of their own day. It would be a lost opportunity if we were to respond to the obsolescence of ancient Stoic physics by pulling in our horns and settling for Minimal Stoicism. If there is any value in the arcane reconstructions of the ancient school for the modern thinker intrigued by Stoicism, it lies in this grand, integrative vision of a good human life, guided by the relentless and unsentimental use of reason in a quest for the best available understanding of the orderly world around us.

Further reading and references

Texts of the ancient Stoics

Brad Inwood and L.P. Gerson, *The Stoics Reader* (Indianapolis, 2008).
A.A. Long and D.N. Sedley, *The Hellenistic Philosophers* (Cambridge, 1987).
Diogenes Laërtius *Lives of the Philosophers* (the best modern-language edition is in French: *Diogène Laërce. Vie et doctrines des philosophes illustres*; Paris, 1999).

For translations of the philosophical works of Seneca the best place to turn is the series published by the University of Chicago Press.

Epictetus *The Discourses, the Handbook, Fragments*, tr. Robin Hard (London, 1995).
Epictetus *Discourses Book 1*, translation and commentary by Robert Dobbin (Oxford, 1998).
P.W. van der Horst, *Chaeremon: Egyptian Priest and Stoic Philosopher* (Leiden, 1987).
A.C. Bowen and R.B. Todd, *Cleomedes: Lectures on Astronomy* (Berkeley, 2004).
Marcus Aurelius, *Meditations*, tr. Robin Hard (Ware, 1997).
Marcus Aurelius, *Meditations Books 1–6*, tr. and commentary by Christopher Gill (Oxford, 2013).

Stoicism in the modern context

Patrick Ussher (ed.), *Stoicism Today*, vol. 1 (Exeter, 2014).

Patrick Ussher with Tom McConnell (eds), *Stoicism Today*, vol. 2 (Exeter, 2016).

Lawrence Becker, *A New Stoicism*, rev. edn (Princeton, 2017; orig. edn, 1998).

Elen Buzaré, *Stoic Spiritual Exercises* (Lulu, 2011).

Thomas Flynn, 'Philosophy as a way of life: Foucault and Hadot', *Philosophy and Social Criticism* 31 (2005): 609–22.

Michel Foucault, *The Care of the Self*, tr. R. Hurley (New York, 1986).

Michel Foucault, *The Hermeneutics of the Subject*, tr. G. Burchell (New York, 2005).

Pierre Hadot, *Philosophy as a Way of Life*, tr. Michael Chase (Oxford, 1995).

Ryan Holiday and Stephen Hanselman, *The Daily Stoic: 366 Meditations on Wisdom, Perseverance and the Art of Living* (New York, 2016).

Donald Robertson, *Stoicism and the Art of Happiness* (London, 2014).

John Sellars (ed.), *The Routledge Handbook of the Stoic Tradition* (London, 2016).

James Bond Stockdale, 'The world of Epictetus', *The Atlantic Monthly* April 1978.

Scholarship and other reading

Keimpe Algra et al. (eds), *Cambridge History of Hellenistic Philosophy* (Cambridge, 1999).

Jonathan Barnes, *Logic and the Imperial Stoa* (Leiden, 1997).

Jonathan Barnes, 'The same again: the Stoics and eternal recurrence', *Method and Metaphysics* (Oxford, 2011), pp. 412–28.

Susanne Bobzien, *Determinism and Freedom in Stoic Philosophy* (Oxford, 2002).

Susanne Bobzien, 'Logic: the Stoics', *The Cambridge History of Hellenistic Philosophy*, ed. K. Algra et al. (Cambridge, 1999), pp. 92–176.

Jacques Brunschwig, 'The Stoic theory of the supreme genus and Platonic ontology', *Papers in Hellenistic Philosophy* (Cambridge, 1994), esp. pp. 118–45.

John Cooper, *The Pursuits of Wisdom: Six Ways of Life in Ancient Philosophy from Socrates to Plotinus* (Princeton, 2012).

Michael Frede, 'The original notion of cause', *Doubt and Dogmatism*, ed. M. Schofield, M. Burnyeat, and J. Barnes (Oxford, 1980), pp. 217–49.

Miriam Griffin, *Seneca: A Philosopher in Politics* (Oxford, 1976/1992).

Ilsetraut Hadot, *Seneca und die griechisch-römische Tradition der Seelenleitung* (Berlin, 1969).

Ilsetraut Hadot, *Sénèque: direction spirituelle et pratique de la philosophie* (Paris, 2014).

Pierre Hadot, 'Une clé des "Pensées" de Marc Aurèle: les trois "Topoi" philosophiques selon Épictète', *Les Études Philosophiques* 1 (1978): 65–83.

Pierre Hadot, *The Inner Citadel: the* Meditations *of Marcus Aurelius*, tr. Michael Chase (Cambridge, MA, 1998).

Pierre Hadot, *Marc Aurèle. Écrits pour lui-même. Introduction générale, Livre I* (Paris, 2002).

Brad Inwood (ed.), *The Cambridge Companion to the Stoics* (Cambridge, 2003).

Brad Inwood and Pierluigi Donini, 'Stoic ethics', *The Cambridge History of Hellenistic Philosophy*, ed. K. Algra et al. (Cambridge, 1999), pp. 675–738.

A.A. Long, *Hellenistic Philosophy* (London, 1974).

A.A. Long, *Epictetus: A Stoic and Socratic Guide to Life* (Oxford, 2004).

Ada Palmer, 'The recovery of Stoicism in the Renaissance', *The Routledge Handbook of the Stoic Tradition*, ed. John Sellars (London, 2016).

Malcolm Schofield, 'Ariston of Chios and the unity of virtue', *Ancient Philosophy* 4 (1984): 83–96.

John Sellars, *Stoicism* (London, 2006).

Simplicius *On Epictetus' Handbook*, tr. Charles Brittain and Tad Brennan, 2 vols (London, 2002).

Index

ONLINE CATALOGUE
A Very Short Introduction

Our online catalogue is designed to make it easy to find your ideal Very Short Introduction. View the entire collection by subject area, watch author videos, read sample chapters, and download reading guides.

SOCIAL MEDIA
Very Short Introduction

Join our community

www.oup.com/vsi

- Join us online at the official Very Short Introductions **Facebook** page.
- Access the thoughts and musings of our authors with our online **blog**.
- Sign up for our monthly **e-newsletter** to receive information on all new titles publishing that month.
- Browse the full range of Very Short Introductions online.
- Read **extracts** from the Introductions for free.
- Visit our library of **Reading Guides**. These guides, written by our expert authors will help you to question again, why you think what you think.
- If you are a teacher or lecturer you can order inspection copies quickly and simply via our website.